Elizabeth Alston's
BEST
BAKING

ALSO BY ELIZABETH ALSTON

Muffins
Biscuits and Scones
Pancakes and Waffles
Breakfast with Friends

JOANNA ROY

Elizabeth Alston's
BEST
BAKING

80 Recipes for Angel Food Cakes,
Chiffon Cakes, Coffee Cakes, Pound Cakes,
Tea Breads, and Their Accompaniments

HarperPerennial
An Imprint of HarperCollinsPublishers

HarperCollins books may be purchased for educational, business, or sales promotional use. For information please write: Special Markets Department, HarperCollinsPublishers Inc., 10 East 53rd Street, New York, NY 10022.

FIRST EDITION

Designed by Elina D. Nudelman

Library of Congress Cataloging-in-Publication Data

Alston, Elizabeth.
    Elizabeth Alston's best baking: 80 recipes for angel food cakes, chiffon cakes, coffee cakes, pound cakes, tea breads, and their accompaniments/Elizabeth Alston.—1st ed.
      p.   cm.
    Originally published: Simply cakes. © 1994 and Tea breads and coffeecakes. © 1991.
    ISBN 0-06-095329-2
    1. Baking.   I. Alston, Elizabeth.   Simply cakes.   II. Alston, Elizabeth. Tea breads and coffeecakes. III. Title.
    TX763.A264   2000
    641.8'15—dc21   99-40942

00 01 02 03 04 ❖/RRD 10 9 8 7 6 5 4 3 2 1

Contents

WITH VERY SPECIAL THANKS TO

RECIPE DEVELOPMENT AND RETESTING:
Mary Adams,
Rebecca Adams,
Louise Burbidge,
Ruth Cousineau,
Sandra Robishaw, and
Miriam Rubin

ASSISTANTS:
Paul E. Bolton and Dionisia Colon

WORD PROCESSING:
Marinella Cancio,
Maria di Martino, and
Nichelle Gainer

JOANNA ROY

Introduction

Not long ago I was sharing cake and coffee with my sister, Jean; her children, Carol and John; and John's wife, Alice, in the kitchen of the farmhouse where I and my three siblings were born. It was the day before the christening of three-month-old Lilly in Alpheton church, where her parents had been married. (Lilly, however, was born in a hospital, not the farmhouse.) Early that morning we had decorated the tiny church (116 seats including extra chairs) with huge bouquets of greens and (of course) lilies. Then back to the farmhouse, and while my sister played grandmother, the rest of us prepared a huge amount of food for the party: tiny mushroom tarts (leek ones, too), open-faced smoked salmon sandwiches, tiny meringues filled with coffee whipped cream, and Scottish shortbread from *my* grandmother's recipe. Carol baked hundreds of chocolate-topped crunchies (a cross between a candy bar and a cookie) and inscribed "Lilly" in white frosting on them. I made literally hundreds of cheese wafers and also decorated the christening cake.

We accomplished a great deal in an amazingly short time, made even more pleasant by good-natured bantering. As we relaxed over coffee and (homemade) cake, John and Alice remarked that nowadays lots of their young friends don't know how to bake (or cook) and buy most of the food for special occasions, such as a christening. They heartily disapprove, and believe that homemade tastes much, much better, is not that hard to do, and leaves you with a feeling of accomplishment. My sister, the grandmother, suddenly giggled: The industrious scene had reminded her of our childhood, when every Thursday was baking day and huge amounts of cakes, scones, shortbread, and other goodies were baked to keep us filled in the coming week. And, she added, we ate all of it!

Although I derive enormous pleasure from all kinds of cooking, there is something magical about baking. After all, you mix powders (flour, cocoa, spices, sugar) and potions (butter, eggs, sour cream, milk), and apply heat (oven). Soon the kitchen is filled with a wonderful smell, and in the oven a wet batter has risen up, taken on a golden hue, and transformed itself into something delicious to eat. The textures (feathery angel food cake, seriously dense pound cake, crumbly streusel, creamy kuchen) are almost as varied as the flavors (think vanilla, chocolate, pear, apple, apricot, hazelnut, pecan, lemon, orange, brown sugar). Yet to bake the simple cakes and tea breads in this book requires little more than basic knowledge, which I have attempted to provide, and attention to detail, such as when measuring ingredients.

When I mentioned this book to a friend whom I met at the Greenmarket recently, he said, "Oh, good. My copy of *Tea Breads and Coffeecakes* is the most stained and tattered cookbook I have." Now there's a nice compliment. May your copy of this book soon become stained from use, and may you derive pleasure from baking for breakfast, dessert, a coffee get-together, and of course, special occasions such as an anniversary, shower, or the naming of a child.

How to Follow a Recipe

Experienced bakers may skip this part.

Read a new recipe all the way through to get a sense of technique and timing. Measure the ingredients.

MEASURING INGREDIENTS

Accurate measuring is important to the success of baked goods. Buy good-quality cup and spoon measures. They are more accurate and last a lifetime.

For dry ingredients such as flours, grains, and sugars, use metal or plastic measuring cups that come in nested sets of 1, ½, ⅓, and ¼ cup. When a recipe calls for ¾ cup of an ingredient, use a ½-cup measure plus a ¼ cup. Do not use a 1-cup measure and guess at the ¾-cup mark.

To measure flour (also cocoa and confectioners' sugar), stir it lightly in the bag or canister. Spoon it into the cup measure until the cup is overflowing. Do not press the flour down into the cup or tap the measure on the counter. Then draw the back of a knife, or other straight edge, across the top of the overflowing cup, sweeping off the excess. (Work over the canister, bag, or a sheet of wax paper.)

To measure granulated white sugar and other flaky or granular ingredients such as cornmeal, oats, and oat bran, scoop the ingredient from the bag or canister with the measuring cup, filling it to overflowing. Sweep off the excess with the back of a knife.

To measure brown sugar, pack it firmly into the appropriate cup measure(s) with your fingertips until it is level with the top.

To measure teaspoons and tablespoons of dry ingredients such as baking powder, baking soda, salt, and spices, dip the exact-size measuring spoons into the can or jar (or if the neck of the jar is too narrow to get the spoon in, fill spoons to overflowing over a small piece of wax paper), then sweep off excess with the edge of a metal spatula. Here's a tip from the *Woman's Day* test kitchen: Fasten a strip of Scotch tape tightly across the opening of a can of baking powder and use the edge of the tape to level off the baking powder.

To measure ⅛ teaspoon, measure ¼ teaspoon, then "cut" through the middle with the point of a knife and push off the unneeded ⅛ teaspoon.

Use a glass measuring cup for liquid ingredients. With the cup on the countertop, pour in the liquid. Bend over and check the amount at eye level.

For semisolid ingredients such as yogurt or sour cream, use cup measures designed for either wet or dry ingredients.

NOTES ON EQUIPMENT

BAKING PANS

Baking pans of any kind work fine, but if you need to buy a pan, go for good, basic light-colored aluminum with straight sides at least 2 inches high. Cakes brown faster in darker pans, sometimes turning too brown before they are cooked through. A nonstick coating makes no sense for a cake baking pan, since it still has to be greased and some of the coating inevitably gets scraped off each time you loosen a cake with a knife. (Even when scratched the pan will still bake okay.) Nonstick or release finishes that are part of the material (and not a "coating") work better, but you still need to grease them. Pans are measured across the inside top. When a loaf pan is called for, I usually specify 9 x 5 x 3 inches. Depending on the manufacturer, any measurements you are lucky enough to find embossed in a pan may not match those given above, but should come close. For example, there's no problem using a pan 9 x 5 x 2¾ inches or even 8¾ x 4¾ x 2¾ inches instead. A better way to measure a pan, except one with a removable bottom, is to fill it with a measured amount of water. In many recipes I've given the approximate yield of the batter (taken immediately after mixing, before any baking powder really gets going). This will enable you to decide if an alternate pan size is suitable. (You may wish to bake the batter in miniature loaf pans, or even muffin cups.) As a general guide, whatever pan you choose, fill it no more than half to two-thirds full. (Bake any extra batter in a miniature loaf pan, custard cup, or muffin pan; baking time will be considerably less.)

Use the following as a guide in choosing alternate pans:

Pan Dimensions	Approximate Capacity	Maximum Batter*
10 x 3-inch round	16 cups	8 cups
10 x 4-inch angel food or tube pan	16 cups	8 cups
9 x 4½-inch Bundt or kugelhopf	12 cups	6 to 8 cups
9 x 5 x 3-inch loaf pan	8 cups	5 cups
8½ x 4½ x 2¾-inch loaf pan	6½ cups	4 cups

*Unless recipe specifies otherwise.

Do not bake angel food cakes in Bundt or kugelhopf pans, because it is extremely difficult to get them out.

ELECTRIC MIXER

For such cakes as pound cakes, which have a large amount of "heavy" batter, use a "stand" electric mixer (comes with its own stand), or a handheld portable electric mixer that's strong enough to handle cookie dough. For angel food cakes, portable mixers are at least as good as stand mixers because you can move the beaters around the bowl while beating the whites, which makes for more evenly beaten whites and is often faster, too.

FOOD PROCESSOR

Several of the pound cake and kuchen recipes include food processor methods. You need an 8-cup or larger work bowl to hold all the batter. (To measure: remove blade, tape hole, fill work bowl with measured cups of sugar.)

MIXING INGREDIENTS

Note which of the three main techniques used is called for. None of them is difficult or requires special skill.

Mix-mix. The dry ingredients (flour, spices, baking powder, baking soda) are mixed in one bowl, the wet ingredients (eggs, melted butter, sour cream, or buttermilk) in another. The wet ingredients are added to the dry and stirred gently until a well-blended batter is achieved. Wet and dry ingredients can be mixed separately ahead of time, but once the baking powder or baking soda is wet it starts to work and the batter should be put in the oven promptly.

Rubbing in. The dry ingredients are mixed in a bowl, then cold butter is cut in with a pastry blender (four semicircular strands of hard wire attached to a handle) or rubbed in with your fingers. The liquid ingredients are then added, and the mixture is stirred to make a well-blended batter or dough.

It takes just 3 or 4 seconds to "rub" fat into four in a food processor, so if you have one, follow the food processor method.

Creaming. Room-temperature butter is beaten with the sugar to incorporate as much air as possible. The remaining ingredients are then added, the order depending on the recipe.

I've given food processor versions for many of the creaming-method recipes. The food processor incorporates little air, so the amount of batter is often considerably less and the baked cake may be smaller in size with a more compact texture. But for speed there is no comparison, and when tasting the food processor and mixer versions of a cake side by side, I have sometimes preferred the closer, denser texture produced by the food processor.

Make sure you have all the equipment and ingredients needed.

If butter at room temperature is called for, get it out of the refrigerator at once. Unwrap it and cut it into small pieces so it can soften while you continue preparations. (Butter can also be quickly softened in a microwave oven; for 8 tablespoons, allow 12 to 15 seconds on medium in a 650- to 700-watt oven.)

NOTES ON BAKING

HEATING THE OVEN

Unless the recipe involves up-front preparation such as peeling fruit, the next thing to do is to turn the oven on so it will be properly heated by the time the batter is ready to go in. Unless a recipe specifies otherwise, bake all cakes and breads in the approximate center of the oven. Before you turn on the oven, check that one rack is in the appropriate place.

GREASING THE PAN

Next, grease the pan if the recipe calls for it, even if the pan has a nonstick finish. Except for a very few recipes in which greasing with butter is specified, these recipes have all been tested with cooking spray—the plain oil kind, not the spray with flour added, although using that shouldn't pose any problem.

Instead of using a cooking spray, you may spread a thin film of butter, shortening, or vegetable oil over the inside of the pan with your fingers or with a piece of paper towel. Fat used for greasing a pan is in addition to any called for in the recipe.

If you bake often, keep a small glass jar or other microwavable container in the refrigerator with some butter in it, ready for melting and greasing. (Keep the jar covered between uses so the butter doesn't pick up refrigerator aromas.)

MEASURE THE INGREDIENTS

With the oven heating and the pan ready, carefully measure the ingredients (see page viii). Then make up the batter and get the cake into the oven.

HOW TO TELL WHEN A CAKE IS DONE

The time it takes for a cake to bake depends on how warm or cold the ingredients were and, therefore, the starting temperature of the batter; also important are the amount of batter, the shape and size of the pan and the material it is made from, and the oven itself. Since each oven has its own unique baking environment (which you learn to work with), the first time you bake a new recipe set the timer for 5 to 10 minutes less than the low end of the range given in each recipe. This first check should be just to make sure everything is going smoothly. The cake should be just about fully risen, or even fully risen, and the batter starting to dry out in the middle. Should a cake seem to be browning too quickly (and some ovens have a tendency to encourage fast browning), cover it loosely with a sheet of foil.

While baking times in a recipe are a guide as to how long a bread or cake will take to cook, the most important factor is your own judgment. You, the baker, are in charge. Use the time given in a recipe as a guide. Set your timer (one with a long, loud ring) for the shorter amount of time in a range. When the timer goes off, look carefully at the cake. It should *look* cooked: no wet patches in the middle (or in the surface cracks). When you *touch* the center, your finger should not sink into uncooked batter. A cooked cake springs back when you touch it. The cake should also *smell* cooked and should be just coming away from the sides of the pan. If those signals seem to indicate "cooked," insert a cake tester—a metal wire on a handle—into the center of the cake. It should come out "clean," that is, without any uncooked batter clinging to it. (You may use a toothpick or bamboo skewer instead of a cake tester, but because it leaves smaller holes, a cake tester is best for an angel food cake.) With certain cakes, little bits of cake or fruit may cling to the pick, but their moistness is different from that of undercooked batter.

If anything, it is better to slightly underbake a cake than to overbake it. A cake baked too long can be dry. Be assured that even very experienced bakers have doubts when it comes to deciding just when a cake is done.

Put the baked cake, still in the pan, on a wire cooling rack on the counter. Exactly how many minutes you leave it there is rarely important, but a minimum of 10 minutes is recommended to give the cake or bread time to firm up and for a slight steaming effect to help free the cake from the pan.

REMOVING THE CAKE FROM THE PAN

Before turning a cake out of the pan, loosen the edges by drawing a thin knife or metal spatula (my baking friends favor an *offset* metal spatula—with the blade at an angle) all around the cake, between the cake and the pan. (If the pan has a nonstick finish use a blunt tool, such as a wooden spreader, that won't scratch the surface.)

Unless the recipe specifies otherwise, turn the cake out onto the rack. A loaf cake will usually slide right out if you turn the pan on one side. Hold the cooling rack upside down on top of a round or square cake pan and turn the pan and rack over together.

More drastic measures should rarely be needed, but if they are, hold the pan (use pot holders) over a gas or electric burner on your stove and rotate the pan just enough to heat the bottom. The heat softens the fat you used to grease the pan and also creates steam that helps free the cake. It's not that easy to heat just the bottom of a pan, but it usually does the trick.

If the cake is to be turned back over, gently hold it in your hands and turn it. Or place another rack lightly on top of the cake, hold on to both racks, and turn them over together (with the cake in the middle).

STORING

Some cakes are best eaten warm. Others benefit from being stored for one or two days at room temperature in order for the flavor to develop. Follow suggestions in individual recipes. Before storing, let the cake cool completely, then wrap it airtight. An easy way is to put the cooled cake back in the pan and overwrap it securely with foil. Or put the cake in a plastic bag (the zip-closure type works well) and squeeze out as much air as possible before you close the bag completely. A plastic storage container is another good choice.

When freezing a cake, proper wrapping is essential to maintain flavor and quality. Plastic "storage" bags are not thick enough. Use bags labeled for freezer use. Most baked goods can be frozen for up to 3 months.

To thaw breads and cakes, transfer them, still wrapped, to the refrigerator a few hours before you want to serve them. Or let them stand an hour or two at room temperature. To thaw a cake or bread quickly, unwrap it and let it stand about 5 minutes at room temperature. Slice it thin and spread out the slices on a rack or countertop. They will be ready to serve in about 10 minutes.

CUTTING CAKES

Cut cakes with a light, sawing motion. A very sharp knife with a thin blade works well, as does a serrated knife. The important thing is not to press down hard while cutting angel food or chiffon cakes.

BAKING AMID CHAOS

Phone calls, kids asking questions, and other distractions make it hard to remember whether or not you have already put the baking powder in the mixture and if you measured 1½ cups of flour or 2½ cups. Here's how to help yourself.

Have *lots* of measuring cups and spoons available (yard sales are often a good source). Take the spoons off their ring; keep them handy in a pot on the kitchen counter.

When you are inspired to bake, quickly read through the recipe, making sure you have not only every ingredient but enough of each.

Before you start mixing the batter, measure every ingredient and leave them in their measuring cup or spoon. (Butter you can leave in the wrapper.) For example, 2½ teaspoons baking powder would occupy two 1-teaspoon measures and one ½-teaspoon measure. (If you don't have enough spoons to do this, put measured baking powder in little heaps on a piece of wax paper so you can easily see you have measured correctly.) If you get distracted, you'll know where you are.

When you have mixed the batter and have put the cake in the oven, immediately set at least one timer and also immediately write down the time you put the cake in. Then, if the timer goes off and you don't hear it, you can at least figure out how long the cake has been baking.

Buy timers with long, loud rings. The kind that you can clip on your belt or hang around your neck may be helpful.

Once you are familiar with a recipe or a technique, prepare a short-hand version. Write the ingredients in black felt pen on a sheet of paper or a large index card. Add an abbreviated version of the instructions. Note the pan size, oven temperature, and baking time. Make one or more photocopies. Tape one inside a kitchen cupboard door, ready for quick access; file the other.

NOTES ON INGREDIENTS

BAKING POWDER AND BAKING SODA

These are not the same and cannot be used interchangeably. Baking soda is pure bicarbonate of soda. In conjunction with an acidic liquid such as yogurt or buttermilk, it is sometimes the only leavening agent in a cake (but more likely in a biscuit or scone).

Baking soda is usually used in recipes to neutralize the acid found in such ingredients as honey, cocoa, or brown sugar.

Baking powder, on the other hand, is used as a leavening, or raising, agent. Double-acting baking powder contains two leavens. One starts to create bubbles when moistened while the other doesn't start to work until heated. The bubbles form and work their way through the batter. As the batter heats and firms, the bubbles are baked in, creating a cake with an open, light texture.

The recipes in this book were tested with double-acting baking powder.

Sifting has been eliminated from the recipes in this book, so when you add baking powder or baking soda to a recipe, make doubly sure there are no lumps. Should any be present, either put the powder in the palm of your hand and mash it smooth with the back of a spoon or sift it into the flour through a strainer (a tiny tea strainer works fine).

BUTTER

For cakes I prefer the fresher flavor of unsalted butter. If you use lightly salted butter, reduce or eliminate any salt in the recipe. You may also use margarine, but please use regular stick margarine or stick butter. Butter/margarine blends in stick form probably would work well, too, but the recipes haven't been tried with them or with "whipped" or "light" or "diet" butter or margarine, often called "spread."

CHERRIES

To pit cherries, you may use a cherry pitter or a large paper clip: Lift the inner curve of metal and bend it back so the clip is an elongated S. Bend the larger end slightly inward so it forms a teardrop shape. Hold the paper clip by the narrow end. Insert the wider end (the teardrop) through the stem hole and under the pit. Pull out the clip and it will bring both pit and stem with it. It takes no longer than 5 minutes to pit a pound of cherries.

CREAM OF TARTAR

Look for cream of tartar (potassium acid tartrate) in the spice section of your market. It isn't a spice but it is packaged by spice companies in the same jars or tins.

Cream of tartar is often called for in recipes where egg whites are stiffly beaten because it stabilizes the egg white foam. I use it in angel food cakes because the volume of the finished cake *depends* on the volume of the beaten whites.

FLOUR

While any grain (including oats, barley, rice, and rye) *can* be ground into flour, when we say "flour" we mean wheat flour. Few other "flours" are widely available and all bake *very* differently from wheat flour. That's because wheat contains a high proportion of gluten, a protein component that, when the flour is mixed with water (and no fat or little fat) and beaten or kneaded, develops a stretchy, elastic quality that's just what you need to make wonderful bread.

Flour varies in its gluten content, depending on the variety of wheat from which it is ground. For most cakes, the less gluten—and the less the gluten is developed in the mixing process—the more tender the finished cake. All-purpose flour is "middle-of-the-road" flour. Widely available, it is perfectly fine for both bread and cakes (use bleached or unbleached). And it may be the only flour you have on hand when the urge to bake a cake strikes. But you may wish to try cake flour, which contains less gluten, and see if you prefer the softer, finer texture it produces in a cake.

Whole-Wheat Flour

I rarely liked the earthy, slightly bitter aftertaste of cakes made with whole-wheat flour—until I tasted cakes made with whole-white-wheat flour. Most of the wheat grown in this country is red wheat, but white wheat (and flour ground from it) is gradually becoming available. It gives you the higher nutritional value of whole-wheat but with a very mild flavor.

NUTS

Nuts taste bitter and acrid when they have turned rancid and are not good for you or the cake. Buy from a source that has a fast turnover and/or that sells nuts in sealed bags.

Once you have opened a sealed package, transfer any unused nuts to an airtight container or a heavy-duty plastic bag specifically designed for freezing food. You can use the nuts straight from the freezer.

To Toast Nuts

Heat the oven. You can use any temperature ranging from 325°F up to 375°F. At 375°F, the nuts toast faster and you should not wander far from the kitchen. At 325°F, toasting is more leisurely and the resulting flavor may be fuller. Spread the nuts out on a baking pan with sides. Set a timer and bake 8 to 10 minutes, or up to 15 minutes at 325°F, shaking the pan once or twice. The nuts are done when they smell toasted and have changed color slightly. The skins of hazelnuts will have split some. Wrap the hot hazelnuts in a dish towel and rub them together with the towel to loosen the skins, then pick out the nuts. (Some skins will cling tenaciously to the nuts and it is fine to use those nuts.)

To save time, toast a double batch of nuts, then wrap and freeze the extra portion.

OIL

Can be olive or a good vegetable oil such as grapeseed, corn, or canola. While making cakes with olive oil may seem radical here in the United States, it certainly isn't in Italy. Try it. Olive oil imparts a lovely flavor without being recognizable as such. Use "pure" or "light" olive oil for most cakes.

ORANGE OR LEMON PEEL

Grating citrus peel has been made faster and easier with the advent of the rasp zester. It's metal, resembles a ruler, and has small, square-edged teeth. Find one in kitchen stores, or cookware mail-order catalogs. Because it is so fast and easy to use, it has made a major, positive change in my personal attitude toward grating lemon or orange peel.

You want to remove just the wafer-thin, bright-colored layer (sometimes called the zest) because therein lie the flavorful citrus oils. Scrub the orange or lemon and wipe dry. Pull the fruit lightly but firmly across the grater in short, sharp strokes. Measure the grated peel, loosely packed, in a measuring spoon. Extra may be frozen. I usually put in a very small jar or plastic container so it is easy to get out. If you have to use a regular grater, use the very small *V*-shaped holes usually found on a four-sided grater, or a small grater sold just for grating citrus peel.

EGGS

You may use a cholesterol-free egg substitute instead of whole eggs. (Check the packages of individual brands for amounts.) You may also use 2 egg whites instead of 1 whole egg.

Eggs are incorporated more easily into a butter-sugar mixture if they are at room temperature. If you are in a hurry, take the eggs from the refrigerator and put them, *still in the shell*, in a bowl of warm water. After a couple of minutes replace the water with warmer water. Even just 10 minutes in warm water will take the chill out of the eggs.

How to Separate Egg Whites from Yolks

Angel food cakes use only egg whites, while most chiffon cakes use yolks and whites, but the whites are whipped separately and folded into the batter.

When egg whites are to be stiffly beaten, make sure that the beaters as well as all bowls and containers they will come into contact with are clean, dry, and free from any grease. Even tiny amounts of oil or grease will prevent the whites from mounding properly.

Have at hand the bowl in which the whites will be beaten, plus a custard cup or other small dish (and another container for the yolks, if you're saving them). If you're separating the eggs for an angel food cake, you'll also need a 2-cup glass measure.

Take the eggs straight from the refrigerator (eggs separate most easily when cold). Give 1 egg a sharp rap on the edge of a bowl to break it open. Hold it over the custard cup and gently pull apart the halves of the shell, letting the yolk slide into half of the shell, and the egg white drop into the custard cup. Carefully slip the yolk into the other half of the shell; if there is still a lot of white clinging to the yolk, slip it back into the other half shell. Then put the yolk into the container you selected for it, or throw it away.

Pour the whites into the cup measure (or into the bowl in which you will beat them). Then continue separating eggs until you have as much as the recipe calls for. The chalazae, the tiny white spiral bands that anchor the yolk, can go in with the whites or not. Should there be a piece of shell in the whites, fish it out. Fish out any specks of yolk, too, using the edge of a shell or a teaspoon. However, if you break the yolk and a lot of it falls into the white, start again. Because if there's even a small amount of yolk in the whites they will not beat to their full potential. (You can scramble the broken egg for breakfast.)

It takes 10 to 12 "large" eggs to end up with 1½ cups of egg whites.

When you have the desired amount of whites, pour them into the bowl in which you will be beating them. Let them come to room temperature while you assemble the remaining ingredients and tools. (If the whites are still very cold when you are ready to beat them, don't worry. The volume will be only very slightly reduced.)

SPICES

Store spices in a cool, dry place (but not in the refrigerator) away from the sun and the heat of your range. Good, full-flavored spices make all the difference in the quality of baked goods. When you open a new jar, write the month and year on the label. Replace ground spices after about a year or add a little extra to the recipe. Whole spices (cloves, cinnamon stick, nutmeg) do not lose their pungency but, except for nutmeg, are impractical to grind for baking. You can buy whole nutmegs and grate them when needed. Use the fine side of a grater or scrape the nutmeg with a paring knife. Allspice is not a mixture of spices but a spice in its own right; whole allspice is a hard, dark brown berry, slightly larger and rounder than a peppercorn.)

SUGAR

Four kinds of sugar are used in this book: granulated white sugar, confectioners' sugar (granulated sugar in powder form), store-bought brown sugar, and homemade brown sugar.

The brown sugar you buy is made by adding a small amount of molasses to granulated white sugar, which is refined from sugarcane or sugar beet. We all know from experience that brown sugar will form rocklike lumps with the slightest provocation. Even a freshly opened package contains tiny lumps, which, while fine to use in most baking, can leave pockets in an angel food cake unless you sift out the lumps. Sifting brown sugar through a strainer (don't try it with a flour sifter) is time-consuming; once sifted, it starts to form a crust if the sugar stands in dry air for even as little as 10 minutes.

However, angel food cakes made with brown sugar have a rich and wonderful flavor. After spending too much time pushing brown sugar through a strainer it occurred to me to add the molasses and granulated white sugar separately.

Here's how: Regular granulated white sugar is beaten into the egg whites in the usual way, as for white angel food cakes. Then, just before the flour is added, a small amount of molasses is beaten in, essentially creating brown sugar right in the batter.

You can make this change in any recipe using the following quantities as a guide. Use mild or dark (sometimes called robust) molasses, not blackstrap molasses, which is too bitter.

Instead of	Use
1 cup brown sugar	1 cup granulated white sugar + 2 tablespoons molasses
1¼ cups brown sugar	1¼ cups sugar + 3 tablespoons molasses
1½ cups brown sugar	1½ cups sugar + ¼ cup molasses

Confectioners' sugar may be used instead of regular granulated white sugar in many cakes, and it imparts a more delicate texture (partly due to the small amount of cornstarch it contains). Usually, 2 cups unsifted confectioners' sugar can replace 1 cup granulated white sugar.

VANILLA

Use pure vanilla extract.

ZANTE CURRANTS

Find these tiny dried grapes next to the raisins in your supermarket. They can be used interchangably with raisins.

These not-too-sweet breads are substantial enough to be breakfast (perhaps with a slice of firm cheese, or spread with Neufchâtel). Most of them can be wrapped in individual slices and frozen, so you can just take out one piece at a time. Since they are raised with baking powder (rather than yeast), they are easy to make. There's also a surprise Savory Sausage Corn Bread.

Breakfast Breads

JOANNA ROY

Spicy Upside-Down Sausage Corn Bread

Makes 6 to 8 Portions

CORN BREAD

1 cup yellow cornmeal

1 cup all-purpose flour

1 tablespoon granulated sugar

1 teaspoon baking powder

1 teaspoon salt

1/4 teaspoon dried oregano
leaves, crumbled

1/4 teaspoon freshly ground
pepper

1 cup milk

1/4 cup olive or vegetable oil

2 large eggs

TOPPING

1 package (12 ounces) pork or
turkey hot breakfast
sausage, thawed if frozen

1 large onion

4 ounces fresh mushrooms

1 ounce (1/4 cup) sun-dried
tomatoes (optional)

CAST-IRON SKILLET, 9 INCHES
ACROSS THE BOTTOM

For a delicious savory start to a weekend breakfast, serve big wedges of this corn bread with fresh tomatoes (small whole, or sliced large). Be careful not to overbake the corn bread; it should be moist.

If using plain (not oil-packed) sun-dried tomatoes, soak them in hot water for 10 minutes, then drain and pat dry with a paper towel. If using oil-packed sun-dried tomatoes, pat dry with a paper towel. Heat the oven to 350°F.

To prepare the batter: Put the cornmeal, flour, sugar, baking powder, salt, oregano, and pepper into a large bowl. Stir to mix well. Pour in the milk and oil; break in the eggs. Beat with a wooden spoon, just until the batter is well blended.

To make the topping: Crumble the sausage into the skillet set over moderately high heat. Cook 4 to 5 minutes, until browned, stirring frequently and breaking up the sausage with a spoon.

While the sausage cooks, chop enough onion to make 1½ cups. Pour or spoon off and discard all but about 1 tablespoon of fat from the skillet. Add the onion to the skillet and cook 2 to 3 minutes, stirring frequently, until translucent. Wipe the mushrooms clean and slice them. Add to the skillet and cook about 1 minute, stirring often. Remove from the heat. Snip or slice the sun-dried tomatoes in strips, stir into the sausage mixture, and spread evenly in the skillet.

Spoon the cornmeal batter over the sausage mixture. Place in the oven and bake until a wooden pick inserted in the center comes out clean and the corn bread feels springy, about 25 minutes. The corn bread should be pale.

Remove from the oven and let stand 5 minutes. Invert the skillet over a large serving plate. Spoon any topping left in the skillet over the bread. Cut into wedges and serve hot.

Whole-Wheat Date-and-Nut Bread

Makes 12 Portions

8 ounces pitted whole dates

1½ cups water

1 large egg

1 teaspoon vanilla extract

1 teaspoon baking powder

1 teaspoon baking soda

¼ teaspoon salt

2 cups whole-wheat flour

½ cup raisins

½ cup walnuts

9 x 5 x 3-INCH

OR 8½ x 4½ x 2¾-INCH LOAF

PAN

A flavorful bread that is also very low in fat. In fact, you can make it practically fat-free by using 2 egg whites instead of 1 whole egg and additional raisins instead of the walnuts.

Heat the oven to 350°F. Grease the pan.

Food processor method (hand and electric blender method follows): Put the dates in a food processor, squeezing each one to make sure there isn't a pit left in. Add 1 cup of water. Cover and process to a coarse puree. Add the egg, vanilla, baking powder, baking soda, salt, and remaining ½ cup water. Process to blend thoroughly. Sprinkle the flour over the surface. Process just until blended. Sprinkle the raisins and walnuts over the top. Turn the processor on/off five or six times to mix in the nuts and raisins but not to chop them.

Spread the mixture in the prepared pan. Bake 40 to 45 minutes, or until a wooden pick inserted in the center comes out clean. Place the pan on a wire rack to cool for 10 to 20 minutes, then turn out the bread and turn it right-side up. Let cool completely. Wrap airtight and store 1 day at room temperature before slicing.

By hand and electric blender: Chop the walnuts with a knife. Mix the flour, baking powder, baking soda, and salt in a large bowl. Add the walnuts and raisins and toss to mix. Puree the dates in 1 cup of water in the blender. Add the remaining ½ cup water, egg, and vanilla, and blend well. Scrape into the flour mixture and stir until the flour is thoroughly moistened. Bake as directed.

Applesauce-Oatmeal Raisin Cake

Makes 12 Portions

1½ cups water
1 cup old-fashioned oats
1 cup dark raisins
½ teaspoon salt
1 cup packed dark brown sugar
1 cup unsweetened applesauce
¼ cup vegetable oil

1½ cups all-purpose flour
1 teaspoon baking soda
1 teaspoon ground cinnamon
½ teaspoon ground nutmeg
2 large eggs
13 x 9-INCH BAKING PAN

Soothing, nourishing, and stuffed with plump raisins. The finished cake is about 1 inch high.

Bring the water to a boil in a medium-size saucepan over moderately high heat. Stir in the oats. When the liquid returns to a boil, stir in the raisins and salt. Reduce the heat and simmer 4 to 5 minutes, stirring occasionally, until the oats are soft and the water is absorbed.

Remove from the heat, stir in the sugar, applesauce, and oil. Cool to lukewarm.

Meanwhile, heat the oven to 350°F. and grease the pan. Put the flour, baking soda, cinnamon, and nutmeg into a large bowl. Stir to mix well.

Stir the eggs into the oat mixture. Add to the flour mixture, and stir just until all the flour is moistened. Spread in the prepared pan and bake 30 to 40 minutes, or until the cake starts to shrink from the sides of the pan and a wooden pick inserted in the center of the cake comes out clean.

Place the pan on a wire rack to cool. The cake is good served warm. Or cool completely, cover tightly, and store overnight at room temperature before serving or freezing.

Whole-Wheat Carrot-Apple Honey Cake

Makes 18 Portions

2 cups whole-wheat flour
1 cup oat bran
2 teaspoons ground cinnamon
1 teaspoon baking soda
½ teaspoon salt
4 large eggs
¾ cup packed dark brown sugar
¾ cup light olive or vegetable oil
½ cup honey
1 pound carrots
1 pound Golden Delicious apples
13 X 9-INCH BAKING PAN

Friends who appreciate the earthy flavor of whole-wheat flour will enjoy this. It isn't very sweet and is very good for breakfast, perhaps with a little cheese or honey butter.

Heat the oven to 350°F. Grease the pan.

Put the flour, oat bran, cinnamon, baking soda, and salt into a large bowl. Stir to mix well.

Put the eggs, sugar, oil, and honey into another large bowl. Beat with a whisk until creamy.

Peel the carrots and shred in a food processor or on the shred side of a four-sided grater. Wash the apples and shred without peeling. Measure 3 cups shredded carrots and 2 cups apples. Stir into the oil mixture. (At this point you can cover and refrigerate the oil mixture overnight. Cover the flour mixture and leave at room temperature.)

Stir the apple mixture into the flour mixture until well blended. Spread the batter in the prepared pan. Bake until a wooden pick inserted in the center of the cake comes out clean, 45 to 55 minutes. Place the pan on a wire rack and let cool completely. Serve the cake freshly baked, or cover and refrigerate up to 3 days, or freeze up to 2 months.

Applesauce–Brown Sugar Bread

Makes 6 to 8 Portions If This Is Breakfast,
10 to 12 If an Accompaniment to Morning Coffee

2 cups all-purpose flour
½ cup packed dark brown
  sugar
1 teaspoon ground cinnamon
1 teaspoon baking powder
½ teaspoon baking soda
¼ teaspoon salt

½ cup walnuts or pecans
1½ cups unsweetened
  applesauce
1 large egg
8½ x 4½ x 2¾-INCH LOAF PAN

A hearty slice of this moist, flavorful, and very low-fat bread makes an excellent breakfast. Or carry a slice to work to enjoy with a cup of coffee. If you want to cut the fat to virtually nil, replace the nuts with raisins or Zante currants (add them at the end so they don't get chopped up) and the egg with 2 egg whites.

Heat the oven to 350° F. Grease the pan.

Food processor method (hand method follows): Put the flour, brown sugar, cinnamon, baking powder, baking soda, and salt into the bowl of a food processor. Process a few seconds to mix well. (Make sure the brown sugar is crushed.)

Add the nuts and process briefly to chop them fine. Add the applesauce and egg. Process a few seconds to mix well.

Spread the batter in the prepared pan and bake until the bread is lightly browned and a wooden pick inserted in the center comes out almost clean, 45 to 50 minutes.

Place the pan on a wire rack to cool for about 20 minutes. Loosen the edges of the bread. Turn it out onto the rack and turn it right side up. When completely cool, wrap airtight and store at room temperature several hours or overnight for flavor to develop.

By hand: Chop the nuts fine. Place in a large bowl and add the flour, cinnamon, baking powder, baking soda, and salt. Stir to mix well. Beat the egg and brown sugar in a medium-size bowl, mashing up any lumps of sugar. Beat in the applesauce until well blended. Add to the flour mixture and stir until well blended. Bake as directed.

◆◆◆

Prune–Oat Bran Bread

Makes 9 Portions

1 cup pitted prunes
2 cups oat bran
2 cups all-purpose flour
½ cup granulated sugar
¾ teaspoon baking soda
¼ teaspoon salt
1¼ cups buttermilk or plain
   yogurt

½ cup light olive or vegetable
   oil
¼ cup unsulfured molasses
1 large egg
9-INCH SQUARE BAKING PAN

The wonderful intense oat flavor and aroma of this bread were inspired by muffins baked by Lawson's, in Washington, D.C. The high proportion of oat bran gives the bread a slightly sticky quality. This bread is good to eat warm for breakfast, about 30 minutes after it comes out of the oven; stored airtight at room temperature, it is even better the next day.

Heat the oven to 325°F. Grease the pan. Oil the blades of kitchen scissors or a knife and snip large prunes into about 12 pieces each, very small prunes into about 6 pieces.

Food processor method (hand method follows): Put the oat bran, flour, sugar, baking soda, and salt into a food processor. Process a few seconds to blend. Add the buttermilk, oil, molasses, and egg. Process 1 to 2 seconds to make a smooth batter. Scrape the sides of the bowl. Add the cut-up prunes. Turn the machine on/off two or three times just to combine.

Scrape the batter into the prepared pan. Bake 50 to 60 minutes, until the bread starts to shrink from the edges, is firm to the touch, and a wooden pick inserted in the center comes out clean.

Place the pan on a wire rack to cool for 15 to 20 minutes. Turn the bread out onto the rack and turn over. Serve warm, or let cool completely, wrap airtight, and store overnight at room temperature before serving or freezing.

By hand: Put the dry ingredients into a large bowl. Stir to mix well. To cut cleanup, measure the buttermilk in a 1-quart measure. Add oil to the 1¾-cup mark and molasses to the 2-cup mark. Add the egg. Whisk with a fork or wire whisk to blend well.

Pour the buttermilk mixture into the flour mixture. Add the cut-up prunes. Stir with a wooden spoon just until well blended. Scrape into the prepared pan. Bake as directed.

Breakfast Fruit-and-Nut Bread

Makes 16 Portions
(Allow 2 Pieces Per Person If This Is Breakfast)

8 tablespoons unsalted butter
1¾ cups all-purpose flour
½ cup granulated sugar
2 teaspoons baking powder
½ teaspoon baking soda
¼ teaspoon salt
2 large eggs
Two 7½-ounce packages
    unsalted farmer cheese

One 6- to 8-ounce package
    mixed diced dried fruit
    (about 1½ cups)
1 cup walnuts, pecans, or
    almonds, chopped
¾ cup milk
1 teaspoon vanilla extract
9-INCH SPRINGFORM PAN

Unsalted farmer cheese (find it near cottage cheese or cream cheese in your market) gives this satisfying bread a complex flavor and damp texture. It also makes it more nutritious. You may use 1½ cups of Zante currants or raisins instead of the mixed fruits.

Heat the oven to 350°F. Grease the pan.

Melt the butter in a small saucepan. Pour into a large bowl; let cool.

Put the flour, sugar, baking powder, baking soda, and salt into a medium-size bowl. Stir to mix well.

Whisk the eggs into the cooled butter. Add the farmer cheese, dried fruit, nuts, milk, and vanilla. Stir to mix well. The mixture will look crumbly and strange, not at all like a batter.

Sprinkle the flour mixture over the fruit mixture. Stir until well mixed. The mixture will still look lumpy and strange, but try not to worry.

Spread the mixture in the prepared pan. Bake 1 hour and 10 to 15 minutes, until the bread is very brown, springy to the touch, and starts to shrink from the sides. A wooden pick inserted in the center should come out moist, with perhaps little bits of fruit or cheese on it, but not totally wet liquid. If after 50 minutes of baking the bread seems very brown, cover it loosely with a sheet of foil.

Place the pan on a wire rack to cool for about 30 minutes. Loosen the edges of the bread and remove the pan sides. Serve the bread warm. Or cool completely, wrap airtight, and store 1 day at room temperature before serving or freezing.

Milo O'Sullivan's Irish Soda Bread

Makes 16 Portions

3 cups all-purpose flour

1/4 cup granulated sugar

1 teaspoon baking soda

1/4 teaspoon salt

1/4 teaspoon ground nutmeg

4 tablespoons unsalted butter, cut up

1 1/2 cups buttermilk, or 1 cup plain yogurt

1/2 cup Zante currants or raisins, or 1/4 cup of each

Additional sugar for sprinkling

BAKING SHEET

When my friend Milo was growing up in Ireland, this bread was baked over an open peat fire in a closed heavy iron "oven pot." Before the dough was put in, the pot was thoroughly heated and then sprinkled with flour. Hot peat was put on the lid of the pot while the bread baked. Milo remembers that his father loved bread and cakes baked over the open fire and thought there was no better way of cooking them. Even in our modern oven, this makes a wonderful dense, chewy bread that will satisfy everyone who craves "real" bread. It's as good with butter for breakfast as it is with cheese for a snack.

In hot, humid weather, start with 1 1/4 cups buttermilk and add more if needed. (If you forget and add too much, and the dough is unworkably sticky, scape it without kneading onto the cookie sheet, sprinkle with sugar, and bake as directed.)

Check that one rack is in the bottom third of the oven and heat the oven to 425°F.

Food processor method (hand method follows): Put the flour, sugar, baking soda, salt, and nutmeg into a food processor; process a few seconds to blend.

Add the butter and process a few seconds to blend. Add the buttermilk and process 2 or 3 seconds until a dough forms. Sprinkle with the dried fruit. Turn the machine on/off two or three times to distribute the fruit without chopping it.

Turn the dough out onto a lightly floured surface and knead just enough to shape into a ball. Put the smooth side up on an ungreased cookie sheet. Pat into a 7-inch round. Sprinkle with about 2 teaspoons sugar. With a sharp knife, cut a deep cross in the dough, cutting a little more than halfway through.

Bake until the loaf is deep golden brown and sounds hollow when tapped, 35 to 40 minutes.

Transfer the loaf to a linen or cotton dish towel placed on a wire cooling rack so that one half of the towel rests on the counter. Cool 5 to 10 minutes, fold the other half of the towel loosely over the loaf, and let cool completely.

Serve the bread on a board. Cut out one quarter at a time and slice it.

By hand: Mix the flour, sugar, baking soda, salt, and nutmeg in a large bowl. Add the butter and cut it in with a pastry blender and/or rub in with your fingers, until the mixture is in coarse crumbs. Stir in the currants.

Add the buttermilk and stir with a fork or wooden spoon until a stiff dough forms, adding a little more buttermilk or water if there is not enough liquid to moisten all the flour. Turn the dough out onto a lightly floured surface. Knead, shape, and bake as directed.

Coffee cakes are informal and homey and often have lavish streusel toppings. Perfect for breakfast, they are also welcome later in the day with a leisurely cup of tea or coffee. Coffee cakes freeze well and are always nice to have on hand.

Coffee Cakes

JOANNA ROY

Pecan Streusel Coffee Cake

Makes 12 Portions

10 tablespoons unsalted butter
2 cups all-purpose flour
1 teaspoon baking powder
½ teaspoon baking soda
¼ teaspoon salt
¾ cup granulated sugar
2 large eggs
1 teaspoon vanilla extract
1 cup reduced-fat or regular
   sour cream

STREUSEL TOPPING
1 cup pecans, chopped coarse
½ cup packed light brown
   sugar
½ cup all-purpose flour
3 tablespoons unsalted butter,
   at room temperature
2 teaspoons vanilla extract
9- TO 9½-INCH SPRINGFORM PAN

This is the perfect streusel coffee cake: a delicate base, lots of topping. You can bake it a day ahead. Or, the night before, mix the dry ingredients and make the topping; leave at room temperature. Combine the wet ingredients and refrigerate. In the morning, turn on the oven and take the wet ingredients out of the refrigerator. When the oven is hot, mix up the batter and you're ready to go.

Heat the oven to 325°F. Grease the pan.

Start the cake: Melt the butter in a medium-size saucepan (or in a bowl in a microwave oven). Remove from the heat and cool slightly.

Put the flour, baking powder, baking soda, and salt into a large bowl. Stir to mix well.

Add the sugar, eggs, and vanilla to the butter; whisk to blend well. Stir in the sour cream.

Put all the topping ingredients into a small bowl. Work with your fingers or with a fork until the mixture is in coarse crumbs.

Add the sour-cream mixture to the flour mixture and stir just until well blended (the batter may be slightly lumpy). Spread the batter in the prepared pan. Sprinkle the topping over the surface.

Bake until a wooden pick inserted in the center of the cake comes out clean, 65 to 75 minutes. Place the pan on a wire rack to cool for 15 to 20 minutes. Loosen the edges of the cake with a knife and remove the sides of the pan. Let cool. If not serving the same day, wrap airtight and store overnight at room temperature, or freeze.

Plum Cobbler Cake

Makes 8 Portions

1 cup all-purpose flour
½ cup granulated sugar
1 teaspoon baking powder
⅛ teaspoon ground nutmeg
2 large eggs
⅓ cup milk
3 tablespoons light olive or
  vegetable oil

1 pound (about 5) ripe black
  plums (such as Black Beauty,
  Black Amber, or Friar)

TOPPING
  2 tablespoons sugar mixed with
  ⅛ teaspoon ground nutmeg
9-INCH ROUND CAKE PAN OR
9- TO 9½-INCH SPRINGFORM PAN

Wonderful served warm, fresh from the oven. Just as good the next day. Measure nutmeg carefully; too much can be overpowering. As the cake bakes, it bubbles up around the plums, hiding most of them.

Heat the oven to 375°F. Grease the pan.

Put the flour, sugar, baking powder, and nutmeg into a large bowl. Stir to mix well.

Add the eggs, milk, and oil. Beat with a wooden spoon to make a smooth, thick, well-blended batter. Scrape into the prepared pan.

Halve and pit the plums. Halve again. Arrange them cut side up on top of the batter. Sprinkle with the nutmeg-sugar topping. Bake until the cake is well browned and crisp on top and a wooden pick inserted in the center comes out clean, 40 to 45 minutes.

Place the pan on a wire rack to cool at least 10 minutes before serving. If keeping overnight, cool the cake completely, cover, and store in pan at room temperature.

Loads-of-Blueberries Coffee Cake

Makes 9 to 12 Portions

4 tablespoons unsalted butter

3 cups (1 dry pint) blueberries

2 cups all-purpose flour

2½ teaspoons baking powder

½ teaspoon salt

¾ cup milk

⅔ cup granulated sugar

2 large eggs

TOPPING

2 tablespoons sugar mixed
with ¼ teaspoon ground
nutmeg

8- OR 9-INCH SQUARE GLASS BAK-
ING DISH

Best served warm, soon after baking, but still very good the next day. Use small berries if you can. Frozen berries work just fine; don't bother to thaw or rinse them.

Heat the oven to 350°F. Grease the dish. Melt the butter in a medium-size saucepan (or in a bowl in a microwave oven). Let cool. Wash and drain the blueberries; spread them out on paper towels to dry, removing any bits of leaf or stalk.

Put the flour, baking powder, and salt into a large bowl. Stir to mix well. Add the milk, sugar, and eggs to the butter. Whisk to blend well. Add to the flour mixture, stirring to blend well. Fold in the blueberries.

Spread the batter in the prepared dish. Sprinkle with the sugar-nutmeg topping. Bake until a wooden pick inserted in the center of the cake comes out clean, 50 to 60 minutes. Place the dish on a wire rack to cool at least 30 minutes before serving.

Simple Sour Cream Spice Cake

Makes 9 Portions

8 tablespoons unsalted butter, at room temperature

1 cup packed light brown sugar

2 large eggs

1 teaspoon baking powder

½ teaspoon baking soda

1 teaspoon ground cinnamon

½ teaspoon ground nutmeg

¼ teaspoon ground allspice

¼ teaspoon salt

2 cups all-purpose flour

1 cup reduced-fat or regular sour cream

9-INCH SQUARE BAKING PAN

A satisfying cake that has a lovely flavor and texture. Sift a little confectioners' sugar over the top shortly before serving.

Heat the oven to 350°F. Grease the pan.

In a large bowl, beat the butter and sugar with an electric mixer on high speed for 3 to 5 minutes, until pale and fluffy. Scrape down the sides of the bowl. Beat in the eggs one at a time. Scrape the bowl. Add the baking powder, baking soda, spices, and salt. Beat on low speed until well blended, continuing to scrape down the sides.

With mixer still running, add about ½ cup of the flour and, without waiting for it to be completely blended in, add about one third of the sour cream. Add the remaining flour and sour cream in the same way. Mix only until blended.

Spread the batter evenly in the prepared pan. Bake until the cake is light gold in color and a wooden pick inserted in the center comes out clean, about 1 hour.

Place the pan on a wire rack to cool for 20 to 30 minutes. Loosen the edges of the cake with a knife and turn it out onto the rack. Turn the cake over and let it cool completely. Serve soon, or wrap airtight and let stand at room temperature overnight.

Cinnamon-Raisin Coffee Cake

Makes 9 Portions

8 tablespoons unsalted butter
1½ cups all-purpose flour
1 teaspoon baking soda
¼ teaspoon salt
⅔ cup granulated sugar
2 large eggs
1 cup plain yogurt
1 teaspoon vanilla extract
½ cup raisins

TOPPING
½ cup walnuts, chopped
⅓ cup packed light brown sugar
2 teaspoons ground cinnamon
9-INCH SQUARE BAKING PAN

Good mid-morning with coffee, or with tea in the afternoon.

Heat the oven to 350°F. Grease the pan. Melt the butter in a medium-size saucepan over low heat (or in a bowl in a microwave oven). Let cool slightly.

Put the flour, baking soda, and salt into a large bowl. Stir to mix well.

Add the sugar and eggs to the butter, whisking to blend well. Whisk in the yogurt and vanilla; stir in the raisins.

Mix the topping ingredients in a small bowl.

To make the cake batter: Add the butter mixture to the flour mixture and stir just until well mixed. Spread about half the batter in the prepared pan and sprinkle with about half the topping. Cover with the remaining batter and topping.

Hold a table knife upright in the pan. Swirl through the batter two or three times to create a marbled effect.

Bake until a wooden pick inserted in the center of the cake comes out almost clean, 35 to 40 minutes. Place the pan on a wire rack to cool for 20 minutes. Loosen the edges of the cake with a knife. Invert the cake onto the rack, then hold a serving plate or another rack upside down on top of the cake and turn everything over together. Serve warm. Or cool completely, wrap airtight, and let stand overnight at room temperature before serving or freezing.

Oatmeal Streusel Coffee Cake

Makes 9 Large Portions

8 tablespoons unsalted butter

1 cup whole-wheat flour

1 cup all-purpose flour

1 cup oat bran

½ cup packed light brown sugar

1 tablespoon baking powder

2 teaspoons ground cinnamon

½ teaspoon baking soda

¼ teaspoon salt

2 cups milk

2 large eggs

2 tablespoons unsulfured molasses, or an additional ¼ cup brown sugar

OAT STREUSEL TOPPING

½ cup old-fashioned oats

½ cup all-purpose flour

¼ cup packed light brown sugar

4 tablespoons unsalted butter, at room temperature

½ teaspoon ground cinnamon

9-INCH SQUARE BAKING PAN

A tall cake, perfect for every day. Two kinds of oats may seem extravagant, but the topping is not nearly so good if you use oat bran instead of big fat flakes of old-fashioned oats.

Heat the oven to 350°F. Grease the pan. Melt the butter; let cool slightly.

Put the flours, oat bran, sugar, baking powder, cinnamon, baking soda, and salt into a large bowl. Stir to mix well.

Measure the milk in a 1-quart measure. Break in the eggs, add the melted butter and the molasses. Beat with a wire whisk to blend well.

Put all the topping ingredients into a small bowl and work with your fingers or a fork until the ingredients are mixed and the mixture is in coarse crumbs.

To make the cake batter: Add the milk mixture to the flour mixture and stir just until well blended. Spread the batter in the prepared pan. Sprinkle the topping over the surface.

Bake until a wooden pick inserted in the center of the cake comes out clean, about 1 hour.

Place the pan on a wire rack to cool for at least 30 minutes before cutting the cake in squares and serving. If not serving until the next day, let the cake cool completely then wrap airtight and leave at room temperature, or freeze.

Chocolate-Marbled Sour Cream Cake with Cinnamon-Almond Topping

Makes 10 to 12 Portions

6 ounces semisweet chocolate (chips or squares)

2 cups all-purpose flour

1 teaspoon baking powder

½ teaspoon baking soda

½ teaspoon salt

8 tablespoons unsalted butter, at room temperature

1 cup plus 2 tablespoons granulated sugar

2 large eggs

1 teaspoon vanilla extract

1 cup reduced-fat or regular sour cream

⅔ cup toasted chopped almonds (see Note)

1 teaspoon ground cinnamon

10 X 4-INCH TUBE PAN WITH REMOVABLE BOTTOM

A treat for those who complain there is never enough topping.

Heat the oven to 350°F. Grease the pan. Melt the chocolate in a microwave oven or in a small, heavy saucepan over low heat, stirring often. Remove from the heat.

Put the flour, baking powder, baking soda, and salt into a bowl. Stir to mix well.

In a large bowl beat the butter and 1 cup sugar with an electric mixer at high speed until pale and fluffy. Add the eggs one at a time, beating after each. Scrape the sides of the bowl. Beat in the vanilla.

Reduce the speed to low. Add about one third of the flour mixture and, not waiting until it is completely mixed in, about one third of the sour cream. Continue until all the flour and sour cream have been added, mixing only until blended.

Spread about half the batter in the prepared pan. Drop melted chocolate in spoonfuls over the batter and spread gently with a rubber spatula. Sprinkle with about half the nuts. Drop the remaining batter on top of the nuts and spread gently. Mix the remaining nuts and 2 tablespoons granulated sugar with the cinnamon. Sprinkle over the batter.

Now, to create a marbled or swirled effect, hold a table knife upright in the batter, almost touching the bottom of the pan. Make zigzag "cuts" through the batter from side to side all the way around the pan.

Bake until a wooden pick inserted in the middle of the cake comes out clean, about 1 hour. Place the pan on a wire rack to cool for 20 minutes. Cut around the edge of the cake (and tube, too) with a knife to loosen. Remove the pan sides. Let the cake cool completely before removing from the pan bottom. Serve within a few hours or wrap airtight and keep at room temperature overnight, or freeze.

NOTE: Buy almonds that are already chopped and toasted. Or buy chopped blanched almonds (almonds with skins removed), spread them out on a cookie sheet, and bake 10 to 15 minutes at 350°F, until medium brown.

Sour-Cherry Almond Crunch Cake

Makes 6 to 9 Portions

1 can or jar (12 to 16 ounces) pitted sour cherries in light syrup or water; or 1¼ to 1½ cups pitted fresh sour cherries (see page xxiii).

1 cup all-purpose flour

⅓ cup granulated sugar

½ teaspoon baking powder

¼ teaspoon baking soda

¼ teaspoon salt

4 tablespoons unsalted butter, cut up

½ teaspoon almond extract

½ cup plain yogurt or buttermilk

CRUNCH TOPPING

¾ cup toasted chopped almonds

⅓ cup all-purpose flour

⅓ cup packed light brown sugar

4 tablespoons unsalted butter, cut up

8-INCH SQUARE BAKING PAN

This recipe works best with pitted fresh sour cherries or with sour cherries packed in a can or jar. (Frozen cherries seem to exude too much liquid.) You need a 12- to 16-ounce jar or can for one cake. The 30-ounce jars that come from Yugoslavia yield enough cherries to make two cakes.

Heat the oven to 400°F. Drain canned cherries in a strainer or colander, then spread out on paper towels to dry further.

Put the flour, sugar, baking powder, baking soda, and salt into a large bowl. Stir to mix well. Add the butter and cut in with a pastry blender and/or rub in with your fingers, until the mixture is in coarse crumbs.

Stir almond extract into the yogurt. Add to the flour mixture and stir with a fork just until the mixture clumps together to form a soft dough.

Spread the dough in a thin layer in the ungreased pan. Scatter the cherries over evenly.

Put the topping ingredients into a small bowl and work with your fingers until well blended. The mixture will be lumpy. Sprinkle the topping over the cherries. Bake until the cake is golden brown and a wooden pick inserted in the center comes out clean, 30 to 35 minutes.

Place the pan on a wire rack to cool. Cut and serve the cake from the pan. Or loosen the edges with a knife before turning the cake gently out onto a plate so the cake is right side up. Then cover with a serving plate and gently turn both plates over together. If you store this cake overnight the almond flavor will develop more fully. But cover the cake loosely or the topping will lose some of its crunchiness.

Spicy Prune Cake

Makes 12 to 16 Portions

1 cup pitted prunes

2 teaspoons instant coffee
   crystals

¾ cup water

1 teaspoon vanilla extract

8 tablespoons unsalted butter,
   at room temperature

1¼ cups packed light or dark
   brown sugar

2 teaspoons baking powder

¾ teaspoon baking soda

1 teaspoon ground cinnamon

1 teaspoon nutmeg

½ teaspoon ground allspice

½ teaspoon ground cloves

½ teaspoon salt

3 large eggs

2¼ cups all-purpose flour

⅓ cup walnuts, chopped fine

13 x 9 x 2-INCH BAKING PAN

Brown sugar and coffee add deep, deep flavor to this moist, richly spiced cake.

Heat the oven to 350°F. Grease the pan. With oiled scissors or knife, snip or cut each prune into 10 to 12 pieces. Mix the coffee crystals with the water and the vanilla.

In a large bowl, beat the butter and sugar with an electric mixer on high speed for 2 to 3 minutes, until pale and fluffy. Add the baking powder, baking soda, spices, and salt. Beat until blended, scraping down the sides of the bowl. Break in the eggs, one at a time, beating after each. Scrape the sides.

With the mixer on low, add the flour about one-third at a time, alternating with the coffee mixture and beating just until blended. Mix in the prunes.

Spread the batter in the prepared pan. Sprinkle with the walnuts. Bake until a wooden pick inserted in the center comes out clean, about 45 minutes. (Be careful not to overbake.) Place the pan on a wire rack to cool. Serve the cake warm. Or cool, cover tightly, and leave at room temperature overnight before slicing or freezing.

Rhubarb Upside-Down Cake

Makes 8 to 10 Portions

1½ tablespoons unsalted butter

About 12 ounces trimmed fresh rhubarb (do not use frozen rhubarb)

2 large eggs

¼ cup granulated sugar

½ teaspoon vanilla extract

Few grains of salt

¼ teaspoon baking soda

¼ cup packed light brown sugar

½ cup all-purpose flour

9 x 1-INCH ROUND CAKE PAN

My mother pooh-poohed rhubarb, the first fresh "fruit" of spring, but next to apples it was my father's favorite fruit. He loved it stewed in red currant jelly for breakfast or dessert. Here the tart flavor of rhubarb makes a lovely contrast with the delicate, mildly sweet cake.

Heat the oven to 350°F. Cut the butter into small pieces and scatter it over the bottom of the ungreased cake pan; let soften while you continue preparations.

Trim the ends of the rhubarb and discard any leaves. (Rhubarb is often sold without leaves.) Wash and dry the stalks. Cut them into 1-inch lengths. You need 2½ to 3 cupfuls.

In a large bowl, beat the eggs, sugar, vanilla, and salt with an electric mixer at high speed for about 5 minutes, until very thick and pale. Beat in the baking soda.

Meanwhile, spread the softened butter thickly over the bottom and lightly up the sides of the pan. Sprinkle the brown sugar evenly over the bottom. Arrange the rhubarb in concentric circles on top of the brown sugar.

Remove the bowl from the mixer. Sprinkle the flour over the surface of the egg mixture. Fold in gently but thoroughly with a rubber spatula.

Spread the batter evenly over the rhubarb. Bang the pan two or three times on the counter to remove any large air bubbles. Bake until a wooden pick inserted in the center comes out clean, 35 to 40 minutes. (Be careful not to overbake. There is very little fat in the cake and it can get dry if overbaked.)

Place the pan on a wire rack to cool for about 20 minutes. Loosen the edges of the cake with a knife and invert it onto a serving plate. Let cool at least 1 hour more before serving.

Tea breads can also be thought of as simple cakes, needing no frosting or buttercream filling. For the most part, they are baked in loaf pans. Made light with baking powder (not yeast) and not too sweet, they are usually served plain, but can easily be dressed up with ice cream or fruit for dessert. Today a tea bread often puts in an appearance as dessert as well as being a sweet accompaniment to morning coffee, or even breakfast.

Tea Breads

JOANNA ROY

Intense Chocolate Tea Bread

Makes 14 Portions

8 tablespoons unsalted butter, at room temperature

1¼ cups granulated sugar

1 teaspoon vanilla extract

2 large eggs

1 cup unsweetened cocoa powder

1 cup reduced-fat or regular sour cream

1 teaspoon baking powder

½ teaspoon baking soda

¼ teaspoon salt

1¾ cups all-purpose flour

Confectioners' sugar

9 x 5 x 3-INCH LOAF PAN

This is good as is or with whipped cream and perhaps sliced fresh oranges for dessert.

Heat the oven to 350°F. Grease the pan.

In a large bowl, beat the butter, sugar, and vanilla with an electric mixer on high speed until pale and fluffy, 3 to 5 minutes. Scrape down the sides of the bowl. Beat in the eggs, one at a time, scraping the sides of the bowl after each.

Turn off the machine. Add cocoa, sour cream, baking powder, baking soda, and salt to the bowl. Mix in at low speed. When the ingredients are well blended, scrape the sides of the bowl. Add the flour; mix only until blended.

Spread the batter in the prepared pan. Bake until a wooden pick inserted in the center comes out clean, about 1 hour and 10 to 15 minutes.

Place the pan on a wire rack to cool for 30 minutes. Loosen the edges of the bread with a knife and invert it onto the rack. Turn the bread over and let cool completely. Sift confectioners' sugar over the top before serving.

Orange–Sour Cream Loaf

Makes 12 Portions

8 tablespoons unsalted butter, at room temperature

1 cup granulated sugar

2 large eggs

1 tablespoon freshly grated orange peel

2 cups all-purpose flour

1 teaspoon baking powder

½ teaspoon baking soda

½ teaspoon salt

1 cup reduced-fat or regular sour cream

9 x 5 x 3-INCH LOAF PAN

The delicate flavor and texture make this a good cake to serve at any time. It is good plain with morning coffee or afternoon tea. For a glamorous dessert, present a slice on a small plate along with 2 or 3 slices of peeled navel orange; accompany with a bowl of whipped cream and a glass of an orange-flavor liqueur or a sweet dessert wine. Few people know or serve dessert wines, but I've always found that even the most skeptical guest quickly revels in the complex flavor a good dessert wine offers.

Heat the oven to 350°F. Grease the pan.

Beat the butter and sugar with an electric mixer on high speed for 5 to 7 minutes, until pale and fluffy. Scrape the sides of the bowl. Add the eggs one at a time, beating after each. Add the orange peel. Scrape the bowl.

Meanwhile, put the flour, baking powder, baking soda, and salt into a bowl. Stir to mix well.

With the machine on low, add about ½ cup of the flour mixture, and without waiting for it to mix in completely, add about one third of the sour cream. Add the remaining flour mixture and sour cream in the same way, ending with flour. Mix only until well blended.

Spread the batter in the prepared pan. Bake until a wooden pick inserted in the center of the cake comes out clean, about 55 to 65 minutes.

Place the pan on a wire rack to cool for about 30 minutes. Loosen the edges of the cake with a knife, and turn it out onto the rack. Turn the cake over and let it cool completely. To store, wrap airtight and keep 1 day at room temperature or freeze.

Dried Pear, Anise, and Walnut Tea Bread

Makes 12 Portions

1 cup water
8 ounces dried pears
3 tablespoons unsalted butter
½ cup granulated sugar
2¼ cups all-purpose flour
1 teaspoon baking soda
½ teaspoon salt

1 teaspoon anise seed
1 large egg
1 teaspoon vanilla extract
1 cup walnuts, almonds, or
    pecans, chopped coarse
8½ x 4½ x 2¾-INCH LOAF PAN

The flavor of this bread gets better and better as it ages, so it is especially good to bake for a large tea party, committee meeting, or reception where you want to have most of the baking done well ahead of time. The slices are mottled brown and white, reminiscent, says one of my friends, of a beautiful calico cat.

Bring the water to a boil while you cut the pears into ½-inch dice (about 1½ cups) and put them into a large bowl. Pour the boiling water over the pears. Add the butter and sugar and stir until the butter is melted and the sugar dissolved. Let cool until ready to use.

Heat the oven to 350°F. Grease the pan.

Put the flour, baking soda, and salt into another large bowl. Crush the anise seed in a mortar, or put the seeds on a board and crush them as fine as possible with the bottom of a glass cup measure.

Add the crushed anise to the flour and stir to mix well. Add the egg and vanilla to the pear mixture, and beat with a spoon until the egg is thoroughly broken up. Add the pear mixture to the flour mixture and stir just until combined. Stir in the nuts.

Spread the batter in the prepared pan. Bake until a wooden pick inserted in the center comes out clean, 55 to 60 minutes. Place the pan on a wire rack to cool for about 20 minutes. Turn the cake out onto the rack and turn over. Let cool completely. Wrap airtight and store at least 1 day before slicing.

Molasses Ginger Cake

Makes 8 Portions

4 tablespoons unsalted butter
1 cup unsulfured molasses
½ cup buttermilk or plain
   yogurt
½ cup packed dark brown
   sugar
2 large eggs
1 ounce crystallized ginger,
   chopped fine (2 tablespoons)

2 cups all-purpose flour
1½ teaspoons ground ginger
1 teaspoon baking soda
8-INCH SQUARE BAKING PAN

Delicious as is for afternoon tea or with cheese for a light snack. Serve warm for dessert with almost-melted vanilla ice cream. The flavor of the cake gets even better if you make it 2 or 3 days ahead.

Heat the oven to 325°F. Grease the pan.

Melt the butter in a medium-size saucepan over low heat (or in a 1-quart or larger measure in a microwave oven).

Remove from the heat; stir in the molasses. Add the buttermilk, brown sugar, eggs, and crystallized ginger. Stir until thoroughly blended, mashing up any lumps of brown sugar.

Put the flour, ground ginger, and baking soda into a large bowl. Stir to mix well. Pour in the molasses mixture. Stir to blend well (a little tricky since you have a lot of wet ingredients and not that much dry). When well blended, spread in the prepared pan and bake until a wooden pick inserted in the center of the cake comes out clean, about 1 hour. Place the pan on a wire rack to cool at least 10 minutes. (The cake will sink a little toward the middle.) Serve the cake warm, or let it cool completely in the pan before storing airtight. Cut into squares and remove from pan before serving.

Quince Ginger Cake

This idea came from Jim Dodge, author of *The American Baker.* Buy about 1 pound ripe quinces. (When ripe, quinces are rock hard, of a yellow hue. Inedible raw, they have a wonderful flavor when cooked.) Peel and core the quinces and cut into rough ¼-inch chunks—enough to make 2 cups. The fruit turns brown quickly; not to worry. Fold the fruit into the batter and bake as directed.

Gretchen's Cranberry-Apple Cake

Makes 12 to 16 Portions
(Up to 28 Thin Slices for a Large Party.)

2 cups all-purpose flour
1 teaspoon baking soda
1 teaspoon salt
1 teaspoon ground nutmeg
1 teaspoon ground cinnamon
2 medium-size Granny Smith
  apples
1¾ cups packed dark brown
  sugar
½ cup vegetable oil

2 large eggs
1 teaspoon vanilla extract
2 cups fresh or frozen cranberries
1 cup pecans or walnuts,
  chopped coarse
10- OR 12-CUP BUNDT PAN OR
10 X 4-INCH TUBE PAN

This recipe comes from my Seattle friend and restaurateur Gretchen Mathers. It makes a handsome cake that's a good "keeper" and is also quite low in fat. It's good alone or with a small scoop of vanilla ice cream. Sift a little confectioners' sugar over the top of the cake just before slicing.

Heat the oven to 350°F. Grease the pan well.

Put the flour, baking soda, salt, nutmeg, and cinnamon into a bowl. Stir to mix well.

Quarter and core the apples (no need to peel). Cut into ¼-inch chunks (you will need about 2 cups).

Put the brown sugar, oil, eggs, and vanilla into a large bowl and beat smooth with a wire whisk. Using a wooden spoon, stir in the flour mixture. Stir in the cranberries, apples, and nuts. The batter will be stiff.

Spread the batter in the prepared pan and bake until a wooden pick inserted in the center of the cake comes out clean, about 1 hour and 5 to 15 minutes.

Place the pan on a wire rack to cool for about 30 minutes. Loosen the edges of the cake and invert on the rack. Let cool completely. It is good fresh; or wrap airtight and store overnight at room temperature before serving or freezing.

Sweet Marsala–Rosemary Cornmeal Cake

Makes 8 to 10 Portions

½ cup golden raisins
½ teaspoon dried rosemary
   leaves, crumbled
¼ cup sweet Marsala or
   Madeira wine
½ cup whole unblanched
   almonds
1 cup all-purpose flour
1 cup yellow or white
   cornmeal

⅔ cup granulated sugar
8 tablespoons unsalted butter
1 large egg
1 tablespoon confectioners'
   sugar,
   or an additional tablespoon
   granulated sugar
8-INCH ROUND CAKE PAN OR
8-INCH SPRINGFORM PAN

This crumbly cake is great with espresso, cappuccino, or a good, strong French-roast coffee. If you've never tried rosemary or cornmeal in a cake before, you're in for a pleasant surprise.

Soak the raisins and rosemary in the wine for 1 hour at room temperature or, covered, up to 24 hours. (Or microwave 4 minutes on high, until the raisins are plump; cool before using.)

Heat the oven to 350°F. If using a cake pan, line it with foil, letting the foil extend over the edge a little so you can lift the cake out.

Grind the almonds as fine as possible in a food processor, or in two batches in a blender. Pour into a bowl. Add the flour, cornmeal, and the ⅔ cup sugar. Stir to mix well.

Add the butter and cut in with a pastry blender and/or rub in with your fingers, until the mixture is in coarse crumbs. Add the egg to the Marsala-raisin mixture, and beat with a fork to break up the egg. Add to the flour mixture. Stir with the fork until moistened and well blended. The mixture will hold together in small clumps. Press it evenly in the pan and sprinkle with confectioners' or the additional granulated sugar.

Bake about 35 minutes, until the cake is a deep golden brown and a wooden pick inserted in the center comes out clean, about 35 to 40 minutes. (Color is the main clue here; the pick may come out clean before the cake is cooked enough.) Place the pan on a wire rack to cool for 10 minutes then lift out the cake by the foil (or loosen and remove the sides of the springform pan) and place it on the rack. Cool at least 30 minutes before serving. Or cool completely, wrap airtight, and store up to 1 week at room temperature.

Food processor method: Soak the raisins and rosemary in the wine. Grind the almonds in the food processor. Add the flour, cornmeal, and sugar. Process briefly to blend. Cut up and add the butter; process just until the mixture is in very small pieces. Add the egg; process briefly to blend. The mixture will come together in a clump. Turn it onto a work surface. Knead in the raisins and any remaining wine. Press into the pan. Sprinkle with sugar and bake as directed.

Chocolate-Orange Crumb Cake

Makes 12 to 14 Portions

2 cups all-purpose flour

1½ teaspoons baking powder

½ teaspoon baking soda

¼ teaspoon salt

8 tablespoons unsalted butter

¾ cup granulated sugar

1 cup plain yogurt or
buttermilk

2 large eggs

1 teaspoon freshly grated
orange peel

½ teaspoon vanilla extract

CRUMB MIXTURE

½ cup granulated sugar

¼ cup unsweetened cocoa
powder

3 tablespoons unsalted butter,
cut in small pieces

2 teaspoons freshly grated
orange peel

9 X 5 X 3-INCH LOAF PAN

Serve this luxurious cake mid-afternoon or as a dessert. It is very moist, almost wet, so have forks handy.

Heat the oven to 350°F. Grease the pan.

Put the flour, baking powder, baking soda, and salt into a large bowl. Stir to mix well.

Melt the butter in a small saucepan over very low heat (or in a large glass measure in a microwave oven). Remove from the heat and stir in the sugar, yogurt, eggs, orange peel, and vanilla. Whisk or stir until well blended.

Put all the ingredients for the crumb mixture into a small bowl and work with your fingertips until the mixture is blended and in small particles.

To make the cake, pour the egg mixture over the flour mixture and stir with a wooden spoon just until blended.

Spread about half the batter in the prepared pan and sprinkle with half the crumb mixture. Cover with the remaining batter and crumbs. To marbleize the crumbs and batter slightly, hold a table knife upright in the batter at one end of the pan. Zigzag from side to side of the pan six to eight times until you reach the other end.

Bake until a wooden pick inserted in the center of the cake comes out moist, but without any uncooked batter clinging to it, about 1 hour. Place the pan on a wire rack to cool at least 30 minutes. Loosen the edges of the cake. Turn out onto the rack and turn over. Let cool completely. Wrap airtight and keep 1 day at room temperature or freeze.

Newmarket Cake

Makes 16 Portions
(Up to 28 If One of Several Cakes for a Party.)

3 ounces semisweet chocolate
   (not chips)
2 tablespoons instant coffee
   crystals
¾ cup water
2 teaspoons vanilla extract
8 tablespoons unsalted butter,
   at room temperature
1¼ cups granulated sugar

4 large eggs
1 tablespoon baking powder
¼ teaspoon salt
3 cups all-purpose flour
⅔ cup pecans or almonds,
   chopped coarse
10 X 4-INCH TUBE PAN OR 9-INCH
SPRINGFORM PAN

A favorite in the horse-racing country around Newmarket, England, this handsome cake is a good "keeper," and it makes a great tailgate cake. It is also good with afternoon tea, or with coffee and a glass of sherry late in the evening.

Heat the oven to 325°F. Grease the pan.

Chop the chocolate into approximately ¼-inch chunks (some pieces will be this big; many will be smaller). Stir the coffee crystals into the water; add the vanilla.

Beat the butter and sugar in the large bowl of an electric mixer on high speed 3 to 4 minutes, until pale and fluffy, scraping down the sides two or three times.

Beat in the eggs, one at a time. Beat in the baking powder and salt. With the mixer on low, add about one third of the flour, then, without waiting for it to be completely mixed in, add about one third of the coffee mixture. Continue until all the flour and coffee mixture have been added, mixing only until blended. Mix in the chocolate and nuts.

Spread the batter in the prepared pan. Bake until the cake is springy to the touch and a wooden pick inserted in the center of the cake comes out clean, 55 to 65 minutes.

Place the pan on a wire rack to cool for about 1 hour. Loosen the edges of the cake with a knife, turn out onto the rack, and turn over. Let cool completely. Serve fresh or wrap airtight and store overnight at room temperature or freeze.

Armagnac, Prune, and Walnut Tea Bread

Makes 12 to 14 Portions.

1 cup (7 ounces) pitted prunes

½ cup Armagnac or Cognac or brandy (for milder flavor, use ⅓ cup spirits plus 2 tablespoons water)

8 tablespoons unsalted butter, at room temperature

½ cup packed light brown sugar

2 large eggs

1 teaspoon vanilla extract

1 teaspoon baking powder

¼ teaspoon baking soda

¼ teaspoon salt

1 cup whole-wheat flour

1 cup walnuts, chopped coarse

9 X 5 X 3-INCH LOAF PAN

Wonderfully boozy. Just right with a cup of tea or coffee, or even a small glass of the same Armagnac you put in the cake. Plan ahead because the prunes need to soak at least 12 hours before you make the cake.

Oil a knife or kitchen scissors and snip or cut each prune into 10 or 12 pieces (very small prunes into 6 or 8). Place in a bowl with the Armagnac, cover, and let stand at room temperature for at least 12 hours—or up to a week in the refrigerator.

Heat the oven to 350°F. Grease the pan.

In a large bowl beat the butter and sugar with an electric mixer on high speed 3 or 4 minutes, until pale and fluffy. Beat in the eggs, one at a time; scrape down the sides of the bowl. Beat in the vanilla, baking powder, baking soda, and salt. Scrape the bowl.

With the mixer on low speed, beat in the flour until almost blended. Mix in the prunes (including any remaining liquid) and walnuts, just until blended.

Spread the batter in the prepared pan. Bake until a wooden pick inserted in the center of the cake comes out clean, 35 to 40 minutes.

Place the pan on a wire rack to cool 20 to 25 minutes. Loosen the edges of the bread with a knife, turn out onto the rack, and turn over. Let cool completely. Serve fresh, or wrap airtight and store at room temperature for up to 3 days. Freeze for longer storage.

Brandied Currant Tea Bread

Makes 12 to 14 Portions

1 cup Zante currants
½ cup Cognac or good brandy
10 tablespoons unsalted
    butter, at room temperature
1 cup granulated sugar
3 large eggs
1 teaspoon baking powder
1 teaspoon vanilla extract

¼ teaspoon salt
2 cups all-purpose flour
1 cup toasted fine-chopped
    almonds
9 x 5 x 3-INCH LOAF PAN

Great with afternoon tea but even better late at night with espresso and Cognac. Try taking a loaf on your next tailgate picnic. This is what a fruitcake should taste like but never does.

Soak the currants in Cognac for at least 1 hour at room temperature—or, covered, in the refrigerator for up to 3 weeks.

Heat the oven to 325°F. Grease the pan.

Electric mixer method (food processor method follows): Put the butter and sugar in a large bowl and beat with an electric mixer on high speed 3 to 5 minutes, until pale and fluffy. Add the eggs, one at a time, beating after each.

With the mixer on low, add the baking powder, vanilla, and the salt. When the ingredients are well mixed, scrape down the sides of the bowl. Add about one third of the flour, and without waiting for it to be completely mixed in, add the remaining flour in the same way. Scrape the bowl. Add the almonds and soaked currants (including any remaining Cognac); mix just until blended.

Pour the batter into the prepared pan. Bake until the cake is lightly browned and springy to the touch about 1 hour and 15 minutes. A wooden pick inserted in the center should come out almost clean but with no uncooked batter sticking to it. Place the pan on a wire rack to cool for 30 to 40 minutes. Loosen the edges of the cake with a knife. Turn it out and turn over. Let cool completely. Serve freshly made, or wrap airtight and store up to 5 days at room temperature, or freeze.

Food processor method: Soak the currants as directed. No need to chop the nuts. Put the butter, sugar, and vanilla in a food processor; process about 1 minute, until pale and fluffy. Add the eggs, one at a time. Scrape the sides of the bowl. Add the baking powder and salt. Process briefly to blend. Add the flour and nuts. Process a few seconds to blend in the flour and chop the nuts fine. Add the currants and any remaining Cognac. Process, using on/off motion, two or three times to mix in the currants without chopping them. Bake as directed.

Sunflower-Seed Tea Bread

Makes 12 Portions

2½ cups (12 ounces) brown-rice flour

½ cup (3 ounces) hulled, but not toasted, sunflower seeds

¾ cup packed light brown sugar

1 teaspoon baking powder

½ teaspoon baking soda

½ teaspoon salt

2 large eggs, or the equivalent in cholesterol-free egg product

½ cup light olive or vegetable oil

¼ cup water

8½ x 4½ x 2¾-INCH LOAF PAN

Friends on a gluten-free diet will especially appreciate the rich flavor of this crunchy-with-sunflower-seeds tea bread. Brown-rice flour (which, unlike wheat flour, is gluten-free) gives a crumbly texture. Be sure the brown-rice flour is fresh and not rancid. (Some stores keep it under refrigeration.) This bread is also delicious served warm and freshly baked for breakfast or with morning coffee.

Heat the oven to 350°F. Grease the pan. (If you're making this for someone allergic to wheat, be careful not to use one of the cooking sprays that contain flour.)

Food processor method (hand method follows): Put the rice flour, sunflower seeds, brown sugar, baking powder, baking soda, and salt into a food processor. Process about 1 minute to chop the seeds fine.

Add the eggs or egg product, the oil, and the water. Process a few seconds to blend well.

Pour the batter into the prepared pan and bake until a wooden pick inserted in the center of the cake comes out clean, 60 to 65 minutes. Place the pan on a wire rack to cool for 20 to 30 minutes. Loosen the edges of the cake with a knife. Turn it out of the pan and turn over. Serve warm. Or cool completely and wrap airtight before storing up to 4 days at room temperature, or freezing.

By hand: Grind the seeds in an electric blender. Put into a large bowl. Add the flour, sugar, baking powder, baking soda, and salt. Stir to mix well. Add the eggs, oil, and water. Stir and beat to blend well. Bake as directed.

Brown-Rice and Nut Tea Bread

Follow the directions for Sunflower-Seed Tea Bread but use ½ cup toasted almonds, pecans, or hazelnuts instead of the sunflower seeds.

These absolutely delicious traditional Middle European treats consist of a soft cookie crust filled with fruit, and sometimes an egg mixture, too, before baking. The crust can be made in seconds in a food processor, and in not much longer by hand. All the recipes call for a 9- to 9½-inch springform pan, so once you have one you can try them all. (Be sure to put the Harvest Tart on your Thanksgiving menu.) When baked, the kuchen are 1½ to 2 inches high. Remove the pan sides and serve the kuchen on the pan base on a larger plate or board.

Kuchen

Blueberry-Raspberry Kuchen

Makes 8 to 10 Portions

SOFT COOKIE CRUST

1½ cups all-purpose flour
⅓ cup granulated sugar
¾ teaspoon baking powder
7 tablespoons unsalted butter
1 large egg

FILLING

4 cups (1½ pints) fresh
  blueberries
1 tablespoon all-purpose flour
⅓ cup seedless red raspberry
  preserves (damson plum is
  good, too)
9- TO 9½-INCH SPRINGFORM PAN

Serve warm for dessert with vanilla yogurt or with sour cream into which you've stirred a little sugar and vanilla. Any leftover kuchen tastes good cold, too.

Heat the oven to 350°F.

Food processor method for crust: Put the flour, sugar, and baking powder into a food processor. Process 1 second to mix. Cut up and add the butter; process 3 or 4 seconds, until the mixture is crumbly. Scrape the sides and bottom of the bowl. Break the egg over the mixture. Turn the machine on/off a few times, until a soft dough forms.

By hand: Put the flour, sugar, and baking powder into a medium-size bowl. Stir to mix well. Cut up and add the butter. Cut in with a pastry blender and/or rub in with your fingers, until the mixture is in coarse crumbs. Add the egg. Stir with a fork or spoon until a smooth, well-blended dough forms.

Spread and/or pat the dough evenly over the bottom and about 1½ inches up the sides of the ungreased pan. Refrigerate while you prepare the filling.

To make the filling: Pick over the blueberries, discarding any stems, leaves, or squashed berries. Rinse and drain the berries; dry on paper towels.

Mix the flour and preserves in a medium-size bowl. Fold in the berries. Spread evenly in the crust. Bake 55 to 60 minutes, or until the crust is lightly browned. Remove from the oven and place the pan on a wire rack. Loosen the edges of the kuchen with a knife and remove the sides of the pan. Let the kuchen cool at least 1 hour before serving. To store, cover loosely and refrigerate up to 1 day. Does not freeze well.

Plum-Walnut Kuchen

Makes 8 to 10 Portions

SOFT COOKIE CRUST

- 1½ cups all-purpose flour
- ½ cup walnuts
- ⅓ cup granulated sugar
- ¾ teaspoon baking powder
- 7 tablespoons unsalted butter
- 1 large egg

FILLING

- ½ cup damson-plum jam or other flavorful plum or black-currant jam
- About 1¼ pounds ripe black plums (such as Black Beauty, Black Amber, or Friar)

9- TO 9½-INCH SPRINGFORM PAN

Make this with any black plums, or with ripe Italian prune plums when they are in season. Expect juice to flow when you cut this kuchen.

Heat the oven to 350°F.

Food processor method for crust (hand method follows): Put the flour, walnuts, sugar, and baking powder into a food processor. Turn the machine on/off a few times until the walnuts are chopped fine. Cut up and add the butter. Process 3 or 4 seconds, until the mixture is crumbly. Scrape the sides and bottom of the bowl. Break the egg over the mixture. Turn the machine on/off a few times, until a soft dough forms.

By hand: Chop the walnuts fine in an electric blender or with a knife. Mix the flour, sugar, and baking powder in a large bowl. Cut up and add the butter. Cut in with a pastry blender and/or rub in with your fingers, until the mixture is in coarse crumbs. Add the nuts and toss to mix. Add the egg. Stir with a fork or spoon until a well-blended dough forms.

Spread and/or pat the dough evenly over the bottom and about 1½ inches up the sides of the ungreased pan. Refrigerate while you prepare the filling.

To make the filling: Stir the preserves in a medium-size bowl. Rinse and dry the plums. Cut each plum into 6 or 8 slices, discarding the pits. Add to the preserves and stir gently to coat.

Spread the plum filling evenly in the crust. Bake until the crust is medium brown, about 45 to 50 minutes.

Place the pan on a wire rack to cool for 10 to 15 minutes. Loosen the edges of the kuchen with a knife and remove the sides of the pan. Let cool at least 1 hour before serving. To store, cover loosely and leave at room temperature or refrigerate up to 1 day. Does not freeze well.

Swedish Apple-Almond Kuchen

Makes 10 Portions

SOFT COOKIE CRUST

1½ cups all-purpose flour

⅓ cup granulated sugar

¾ teaspoon baking powder

⅛ teaspoon (or slightly less)
ground cardamom, or ½
teaspoon vanilla extract

7 tablespoons unsalted butter

1 large egg

ALMOND FILLING

½ cup blanched or unblanched
almonds (whole, chopped,
or slivered)

½ cup granulated sugar

3 tablespoons all-purpose flour

1 large egg

2 tablespoons unsalted butter

⅛ teaspoon (or slightly less)
ground cardamom, or 2 teaspoon vanilla extract

3 medium-size or 4 small
Golden Delicious or other
aromatic apples

Confectioners' sugar

9- TO 9½-INCH SPRINGFORM PAN

The soft cookie crust is filled with apples and an almond mixture. Heat the oven to 350°F.

Food processor method for crust (hand method follows): Put the flour, sugar, baking powder, and cardamom (if using) into a food processor; process 1 second to mix. Cut up and add the butter. Process 3 or 4 seconds, until the mixture is crumbly. Scrape the sides and bottom of the bowl. Break the egg over the mixture; sprinkle with vanilla (if using). Turn the machine on/off a few times until a soft dough forms.

By hand: Put the flour, sugar, baking powder, and cardamom (if using) into a medium-size bowl. Stir to mix well. Cut up and add the butter. Cut in with a pastry blender and/or rub in with your fingers, until the mixture is in coarse crumbs. Add the egg and vanilla (if using). Stir with a fork or spoon until a smooth, well-blended dough forms.

Spread and/or pat the dough evenly over the bottom and about 1½ inches up the sides of the ungreased pan. Refrigerate while you prepare the filling.

To make the filling: Put the almonds, sugar, and flour in a blender or food processor. Process about 1 minute, until the almonds are ground fine. Add the egg, butter, and cardamom or vanilla; process until well blended (the mixture will not be absolutely smooth).

Peel, quarter, and core the apples. One at a time, hold each quarter on a cutting board with a cut side down. Using a small, sharp knife, slice each quarter thin, working from stem to blossom end, but not cutting quite all the way through to where the core was. (Each quarter will be sliced, but the slices won't come apart.)

Pour the almond mixture into the cookie crust. Arrange apple quarters side by side, slightly overlapping, in the almond mixture, core sides down. Bake 60 to 65 minutes, until the crust is very golden and the apples are beginning to brown. Place the pan on a wire rack. Loosen the edges of the kuchen with a knife and remove the sides of the pan. Let cool at least 1 hour. Or cool completely, cover, and refrigerate. This kuchen keeps several days but does not freeze well. Sprinkle with confectioners' sugar before serving.

Pear-Almond Kuchen

Follow the directions for Swedish Apple-Almond Kuchen but omit the cardamom—and, of course, the apples. Peel, quarter, and core 2 medium-size firm, ripe Bartlett pears. Cut into ½-inch chunks (you need 2 cups). Put into the cookie crust and pour Almond Filling over the top. Bake as directed.

Sour Cherry–Almond Kuchen

Follow the recipe for Swedish Apple-Almond Kuchen but omit the apples, cardamom, and vanilla. Instead, add ¼ teaspoon almond extract to both crust and filling. Pit enough sour cherries (about 12 ounces) to make 2 cups. Or thoroughly drain a 12- or 16-ounce can or jar of pitted sour cherries. Put the cherries in the crust and pour Almond Filling over them. Bake as directed.

Vanilla–Pear Custard Kuchen

Makes 8 to 10 Portions

SOFT COOKIE CRUST
- 1½ cups all-purpose flour
- ⅓ cup granulated sugar
- ¾ teaspoon baking powder
- 7 tablespoons unsalted butter
- 1 large egg
- ½ teaspoon vanilla extract

FILLING
- 3 ripe Bartlett pears (about 6 ounces each)
- ½ cup reduced-fat or regular sour cream
- 1 large egg
- ¼ cup granulated sugar
- 1 tablespoon all-purpose flour
- 1 teaspoon vanilla extract
- 9- TO 9½-INCH SPRINGFORM PAN

Be sure to use ripe, aromatic pears. Bartletts work well.
Heat the oven to 350°F.

Food processor method for crust (hand method follows): Put the flour, sugar, and baking powder into a food processor. Process 1 second to mix. Cut up and add the butter. Process 3 or 4 seconds, until the mixture is crumbly. Scrape the sides and bottom of the bowl. Break the egg over the mixture. Sprinkle with vanilla. Turn the machine on/off a few times until a soft dough forms.

Spread or pat the dough evenly over the bottom and 1 to 1½ inches up the sides of the pan.

By hand: Put flour, sugar, and baking powder into a medium-size bowl. Stir to mix well. Cut up and add the butter. Cut in with a pastry blender and/or rub in with your fingers, until the mixture is in coarse crumbs. Add the egg and vanilla. Stir with a fork or spoon until a smooth, well-blended dough forms.

To make the filling: Peel the pears, quarter lengthwise, and remove the cores. Slice the pears thin from stem end to blossom end. Scatter the fruit over the crust. Bake 30 minutes.

Measure the sour cream in a 2-cup or larger measure. Add the remaining ingredients and whisk to blend. Drizzle over the fruit. Shake the pan gently to settle the custard. Bake 18 to 20 minutes longer, until the custard is no longer liquid in the center (it should be creamy). Place the pan on a wire rack to cool for 5 minutes. Loosen the edges of the kuchen with a knife and remove the sides of the pan. Let cool completely before serving. Refrigerate after 1 hour. Leftovers are very good cold.

Vanilla–Apple Custard Kuchen

Follow directions for Vanilla–Pear Custard Kuchen but use 3 medium-size Golden Delicious or other aromatic apples instead of the pears. Bake as directed.

Lemony Apple Kuchen

Makes 8 to 10 Portions

SOFT COOKIE CRUST
  1½ cups all-purpose flour
  ⅓ cup granulated sugar
  ¾ teaspoon baking powder
  7 tablespoons unsalted butter
  1 large egg

FILLING
  1 large egg
  ¼ cup granulated sugar
  1 tablespoon all-purpose flour
  1 teaspoon freshly grated
    lemon peel
  1¼ to 1½ pounds Granny
    Smith or other tart apples
9- TO 9½-INCH SPRINGFORM PAN

The flavor is delicious but the kuchen looks rather plain, so sift a little confectioners' sugar over the top just before serving.

Food processor method for crust (hand method follows): Put the flour, sugar, and baking powder into a food processor. Process 1 second to mix. Cut up and add the butter; process 3 or 4 seconds, until the mixture is crumbly. Scrape the sides and bottom of the bowl. Break the egg over the mixture. Process a few seconds, until a soft dough forms.

By hand: Put the flour, sugar, and baking powder into a medium-size bowl. Stir to mix well. Cut up and add the butter. Cut in with a plastry blender and/or rub in with your fingers, until the mixture is in coarse crumbs. Add the egg. Stir with a fork or spoon until a smooth, well-blended dough forms.

Spread and/or pat the dough evenly over the bottom and about 1½ inches up the sides of the ungreased pan. Refrigerate while you prepare the filling. Heat the oven to 350° F.

To make the filling: Put the egg, sugar, flour, and lemon peel into a medium-size bowl. Whisk to blend well.

Wash the apples. Shred them either in a food processor or on the coarse side of a grater, shredding them down to the core (no need to peel or cut up the apples first). As each apple is shredded, add the shreds to the egg mixture and stir to coat.

Spread the filling evenly in the kuchen crust. Bake until the crust is medium brown around the edges, about 45 minutes. Place the pan on a wire rack. Loosen the edges of the kuchen with a knife and remove the sides of the pan. Let cool at least 2 hours before serving. To store, cover and refrigerate up to 2 days. Does not freeze well.

Harvest Tart

Makes 8 Portions

SOFT COOKIE CRUST
1 cup hazelnuts
1/2 cup granulated sugar
1 1/2 cups all-purpose flour
3/4 teaspoon baking powder
7 tablespoons unsalted butter
1 large egg

TOPPING
1/2 cup reserved hazelnut-
  sugar mixture

2 tablespoons unsalted butter
2 tablespoons all-purpose flour

FILLING
1 1/2 cups water
One 11-ounce package mixed
  dried fruits (almost 3 cups),
  or your own combination
2 tablespoons lemon juice
1 tablespoon brandy
9- TO 9 1/2-INCH SPRINGFORM PAN

A divine combination of nuts and dried fruits, this kuchen makes a perfect dessert or coffee cake any time during the fall or winter holiday season. Try it for Thanksgiving. The flavor is even better the next day, so you can easily make this ahead. Instead of using already-mixed dried fruits, you can mix your own, using dried apples, apricots, prunes, and, if you wish, pears and raisins. Prepare the filling while the nuts toast.

Heat the oven to 350°F. Spread the hazelnuts in a baking pan and bake 10 to 15 minutes, shaking the pan once or twice, until the nuts smell toasty and turn light brown.

Wrap the nuts in a dish towel and rub to loosen the skins. Pick out the nuts; some skins will adhere—not to worry.

Food processor method for crust: Process the nuts and the sugar until the nuts are ground fine. Remove 1/2 cup of the mixture and save for the topping.

Add the flour and baking powder to the work bowl. Process a few seconds to mix. Cut up and add the butter. Process 3 or 4 seconds until the mixture is crumbly. Scrape the sides and bottom of the bowl. Break the egg over the mixture. Turn the machine on/off a few times until a soft dough forms.

Spread and/or pat the dough evenly over the bottom and about 1½ inches up the sides of the ungreased pan. Fill right away or refrigerate.

To make the filling: Snip or cut the fruit into ½-inch pieces. Bring the water to a boil in a medium-size saucepan. Add the fruit and simmer 8 to 10 minutes, until most of the liquid has been absorbed. Remove from the heat. Stir in the lemon juice and brandy. Let cool 10 minutes.

To make the topping: Put the reserved ½ cup nuts and sugar back into the food processor. Add the butter and flour. Process 1 or 2 seconds, until crumbly.

Spread the warm filling in the crust. Sprinkle with the topping. Bake about 40 minutes, until the crust is medium brown. Place the pan on a wire rack to cool for 15 to 20 minutes. Loosen the edges of the kuchen with a knife and remove the sides of the pan. Serve the tart warm. Or cool completely, cover loosely, and store overnight at room temperature.

By hand and electric blender: Grind the toasted hazelnuts in the blender in one or two batches. Put them into a large bowl. Add the sugar and mix well. Remove ½ cup of the mixture and reserve for the topping. To the nuts and sugar remaining in the bowl, add the 1½ cups flour and the baking powder. Stir to mix well. Cut up and add the butter. Cut in with a pastry blender and/or rub in with your fingers, until the mixture is in coarse crumbs. Add the egg. Stir with a fork or wooden spoon until a firm dough forms. Line the pan with the dough and prepare the filling as above. Put the reserved ½ cup sugar and nuts into a small bowl. Add the butter and flour for the topping. Work with your fingers or a fork until well blended and crumbly. Sprinkle the topping over the fruit and bake as directed.

Peaches-and-Cream Kuchen

Makes 12 to 16 Portions

SOFT COOKIE CRUST
  2 cups all-purpose flour
  ½ cup granulated sugar
  1 teaspoon baking powder
  10 tablespoons unsalted butter
  2 large eggs
  2 teaspoons vanilla extract

FILLING
  2 pounds ripe peaches or nec-
    tarines (6 medium-size), or
    one 29-ounce can and one
    16-ounce can sliced peaches
    packed in light syrup, fruit
    juice, or heavy syrup, thor-
    oughly drained

1 cup reduced-fat or regular
  sour cream
2 large eggs
⅓ cup granulated sugar
  (reduce to ¼ cup if using
  canned peaches)
2 tablespoons all-purpose flour
1 tablespoon vanilla extract
13 x 9 x 2-INCH BAKING PAN OR
GLASS OR CERAMIC DISH

Very easy to make and great to take to a meeting or morning coffee gathering. It's also very good made with fresh nectarines. However, any time you can't buy really good, ripe fresh peaches (not
woolly textured ones), use canned peaches. You can count on them
to be consistent.

Heat the oven to 350°F.

Food processor method for crust (hand method follows): Put flour,
sugar, and baking powder into a food processor. Process 1 to 2 seconds to mix. Cut up and add the butter. Process a few seconds, until
the mixture is crumbly. Scrape the bottom and sides of the bowl.

Break the eggs over the mixture. Sprinkle with vanilla. Process a few seconds longer, until a soft dough forms.

By hand: Mix the flour, sugar, and baking powder in a medium-size bowl. Cut up and add the butter. Cut in with pastry blender and/or rub in with your fingers, until the mixture is in coarse crumbs. Add the eggs and vanilla. Stir with a fork until a smooth, well-blended dough forms.

Spread and pat the dough evenly over the bottom of the ungreased pan. (Dampen or lightly flour your hands if the dough is very sticky.) Refrigerate while you prepare the fruit.

To make the filling: If using fresh peaches, dip 2 or 3 at a time into a saucepan of boiling water; leave 15 to 20 seconds, then remove with a slotted spoon and rinse in cold water to stop them from cooking. Pull off the peel. Cut each peach or nectarine (no need to peel nectarines) into 10 to 12 wedges. Arrange in 4 or 5 crosswise rows on top of the dough (5 will be a tight fit). If using canned peaches, drain thoroughly on paper towels before arranging on the dough.

Bake 30 minutes. Meanwhile, measure sour cream in a 2-cup or larger measure. Add the remaining filling ingredients and whisk to blend well.

Drizzle the custard over the peaches. It won't seem like enough but don't worry. Shake the pan back and forth gently until the custard is in an even layer. Bake 20 to 22 minutes longer, until the custard is set in the middle (it will firm more on cooling). Place the pan on a wire rack to cool. Do not leave the kuchen at room temperature for more than 1 hour; cover and refrigerate up to 3 days. Let come to room temperature before serving. Do not freeze. Cut into squares and serve from the pan.

These delicate cakes are virtually fat-free, because they are made from only the white part of the egg. Do not expect to end up with quite the high-and-haughty look of a bakery cake or one made from a mix. I love intense flavors, and once you start loading angel food cake batter with (weighty) flavoring ingredients, you lose volume. But I think you'll agree that the results are worth it. A simple one to try first is Brown Sugar Angel Food Cake, page 80.

Angel Food Cakes

JOANNA ROY

Each time I make an angel food cake I'm amazed at how few ingredients are required and how little time it takes to prepare the batter.

Traditionally, angel food cakes are baked in a tube pan—a tall, slope-sided pan with a hollow tube up the center. However, bakeries often bake angel food cakes in loaf pans. In their book *New Orleans*, Lee Bailey and Ella Brennan call for a plain round 10 x 3-inch pan. My first thought was—a mistake! But the photograph showed a cake with no hole in the middle, which convinced me to try the pan called for. I liked the result very much. It looks more like a regular cake, and more contemporary than a tube-pan cake. Here, the choice is yours. The pan, by the way, can be more than 3 inches high (as a springform pan, for example, commonly is). It just shouldn't be less, because although the finished cake will be only about 2 to 3 inches high, the batter often rises higher than that during baking. Most of the angel food cakes in this book can also be baked in a 9-inch springform pan. This works fine but, because the batter will be deeper, you will need to count on 5 to 10 minutes additional baking time.

Here's a plan of action for angel food cakes:

- Make sure you have all the ingredients and tools you will need.
- Make sure the bowl in which you plan to make the batter is absolutely clean and grease-free (the beaters, too). Use a metal or glass bowl, not a plastic bowl.
- Take the eggs out of the refrigerator and separate the yolks from the whites (see page xxviii). You won't need the yolks. Put the whites in the bowl in which you plan to make the batter.
- Turn on the oven, first checking that one rack is in the middle position. Prepare the pan (if any preparation is needed).
- Measure all the ingredients and have all the tools at hand.
- Start making the batter and do not stop until the cake is in the oven.

- Beat the whites at medium speed and *not* until they are as stiff as possible. To test, lift some of the whites out with a spatula. A long tip should pull out where you lifted from. When properly beaten, the long tip of beaten whites should flop over, not stand stiffly upright. (If too stiff, however, just continue with the recipe. It will be a little tricky to fold in the flour mixture and the volume will be slightly less, but the flavor won't be affected.)
- When the cake tests done, let it cool, upside down, on a cooling rack for at least 1 hour. (Several hours is fine, if more convenient.)

Although the techniques are essentially the same, almost every cake has been written as a separate recipe, because I hate trying to figure out "variations" as much as anyone.

Brown Sugar Angel Food Cake

12 to 16 Portions

1½ cups egg whites (see page xxviii if you need help)
1¼ cups granulated sugar
1¼ cups cake flour, or 1 cup all-purpose flour
1½ teaspoons cream of tartar
¼ cup mild or dark molasses

Confectioners' sugar (optional)
10 x 4-INCH TUBE PAN OR
9- TO 10-INCH ROUND CAKE PAN
WITH SIDES AT LEAST 3 INCHES
HIGH (A REMOVABLE BOTTOM IS
HELPFUL)

Enjoy the deep, rich flavor alone, or with a small scoop of vanilla or butter pecan ice cream (try mango sorbet in the summertime).

Check that one rack is in the middle of the oven and heat the oven to 325°F.

Pour the egg whites into the bowl in which you will be making the batter.

If the pan has a removable bottom, do nothing to it. If it does not, lightly butter the bottom (page xx). Line the bottom with wax paper or parchment paper cut to fit, and lightly butter the paper.

Thoroughly mix ¼ cup of the sugar and the flour in a small bowl. Have all the ingredients and tools at hand.

Beat the egg whites with an electric mixer on medium speed for about 2 minutes, until frothy and well broken up. Add the cream of tartar and increase the speed to medium-high. Beat until the whites lose their yellow cast, greatly increase in volume, and start to turn white.

With the mixer running, slowly sprinkle the remaining 1 cup sugar over the whites. Beat until the whites become very thick, very glossy, and white, and the beaters leave a deep trail. Depending on the mixer, this need take only about 3 minutes total.

Reduce the speed to the lowest possible. Pour in the molasses. Beat a few seconds, scraping the sides of the bowl with a rubber spatula to make sure all the molasses is incorporated.

Quickly sprinkle the flour-sugar mixture over the whites. As soon as it is all added but not completely mixed in, stop the machine and remove the bowl.

With a rubber spatula or a large metal spoon, complete mixing in the flour by folding or gently stirring. Stop just as soon as the flour seems blended in.

With a rubber spatula, scrape the batter (9 to 10 cups) into the pan and spread evenly. Inscribe a circle deep in the batter to release any large air bubbles.

Bake until no moist patches remain in the surface cracks, the cake springs back when touched, and a cake tester inserted in the center comes out clean—about 50 minutes for a 10 x 3-inch pan, 1 hour for a tube pan. Turn the cake pan upside down on a wire rack. Let cool completely.

Loosen the edges (and tube) with a knife. Turn out the cake, loosen and remove the pan bottom, or peel off the paper. Store airtight 1 day at room temperature before serving or freezing. If you wish, sift confectioners' sugar over the top before serving.

Spicy Brown Sugar Angel Food Cake

An excellent everyday cake that can even put in a welcome appearance at a late breakfast. It doesn't *need* a sauce, but for a special occasion such as Thanksgiving, try Nutmeg-Honey Whipped Cream (page 161), Caramel Apples (page 165), or Pineapple–Golden Raisin Sauce (page 162).

Use the same ingredients and pan as for Brown Sugar Angel Food Cake (page 80), plus 1 teaspoon ground cinnamon, ½ teaspoon ground nutmeg, and ½ teaspoon ground cloves.

Follow the directions for Brown Sugar Angel Food Cake, adding the spices to the egg whites while you're adding the last spoonful or two of sugar. Proceed and bake as directed.

Fresh Raspberry Angel Food Cake

12 Portions

1½ cups egg whites (see page
    xxviii if you need help)
1–2 cups (½ to 1 pint) fresh
    red raspberries
1¼ cups granulated sugar
1¼ cups cake flour, or 1 cup
    all-purpose flour
1½ teaspoons cream of tartar
¼ cup mild or dark molasses

10 x 4-INCH TUBE PAN OR
9- TO 10-INCH ROUND CAKE PAN
WITH SIDES AT LEAST 3 INCHES
HIGH (A REMOVABLE BOTTOM IS
HELPFUL)

Enjoy this unbelievably good cake with cappuccino or tea and no other distractions. This cake is best served the day it is made, but if you're keeping it longer, wrap it tightly and refrigerate it.

Check that one rack is in the middle of the oven and heat the oven to 325°F.

Pour the egg whites into the bowl in which you will be making the batter.

If the pan has a removable bottom, do nothing to it. If it does not, lightly butter the bottom (page xx). Line the bottom with wax paper or parchment paper cut to fit, and lightly butter the paper.

Do not wash the raspberries; just pick out any very squashed or (of course) moldy ones.

Thoroughly mix ¼ cup of the sugar and the flour in a small bowl. Have all the ingredients and tools at hand.

Beat the egg whites with an electric mixer on medium speed for about 2 minutes, until frothy and well broken up. Add the cream of tartar and increase the speed to medium-high. Beat until the whites lose their yellow cast, greatly increase in volume, and start to turn white.

With the mixer running, slowly sprinkle the remaining 1 cup sugar over the whites. Beat until the whites become very thick, very glossy, and white, and the beaters leave a deep trail. Depending on the mixer, this need take only about 3 minutes total.

Reduce the speed to the lowest possible. Pour in the molasses. Beat a few seconds, scraping the sides of the bowl with a rubber spatula to make sure all the molasses is incorporated.

Quickly sprinkle the flour-sugar mixture over the whites, beating lightly. As soon as it is all added but not completely mixed in, stop the machine and remove the bowl.

Sprinkle the raspberries over the batter. With a rubber spatula or a large metal spoon, complete mixing in the flour along with the raspberries by folding or gently stirring. Stop just as soon as the flour seems blended in.

With a rubber spatula, scrape the batter (9 to 10 cups) into the pan and spread evenly. Inscribe a circle deep in the batter to release any large air bubbles.

Bake until no moist patches remain in the surface cracks, the cake springs back when touched, and a cake tester inserted in the center comes out clean—about 50 minutes for a 10 x 3-inch pan, 1 hour for a tube pan. Turn the cake pan upside down on a wire rack. Let cool completely.

Loosen the edges (and tube) with a knife. Turn out the cake, loosen and remove the pan bottom, or peel off the paper.

Caramel-Coffee Angel Food Cake

12 to 16 Portions

1½ cups egg whites (see page
   xxviii if you need help)
½ cup toasted chopped
   almonds (page xxv)
1¼ cups granulated sugar
1 cup all-purpose flour, or 1¼
   cups cake flour
1½ teaspoons cream of tartar

1 tablespoon instant coffee
   powder, preferably espresso
1 teaspoon vanilla extract
⅓ cup mild molasses
Confectioners' sugar
9- TO 10-INCH ROUND CAKE PAN
WITH SIDES AT LEAST 3 INCHES
HIGH

You can't add nuts to an angel food cake (their oil causes the beaten whites to collapse), but you can put them on the bottom of the pan. They taste wonderful with the cake even though they make cutting it a little tricky. Try serving the cake *nuts down*. Slice it with a sawing motion; when you come to the nuts cut straight down.

Check that one rack is in the middle of the oven and heat the oven to 325°F.

Pour the egg whites into the bowl in which you will be making the batter.

Lightly butter the bottom of the pan (page xx). Line with wax paper or parchment paper cut to fit, and lightly butter the paper. Sprinkle the toasted chopped almonds evenly over the bottom of the pan.

Thoroughly mix ¼ cup of the sugar and the flour in a small bowl. Have all the ingredients and tools at hand.

Beat the egg whites with an electric mixer on medium speed for about 2 minutes, until frothy and well broken up. Add the cream of tartar and increase the speed to medium-high. Beat until the whites

lose their yellow cast, greatly increase in volume, and start to turn white. Add the instant coffee powder and the vanilla.

With the mixer running, slowly sprinkle the remaining 1 cup sugar over the whites. Beat until the whites become very thick, very glossy, and white, and the beaters leave a deep trail. Depending on the mixer, this need take only about 3 minutes total.

Reduce the speed to the lowest possible. Pour in the molasses. Beat a few seconds, scraping the sides of the bowl with a rubber spatula to make sure all the molasses is incorporated.

Quickly sprinkle the flour-sugar mixture over the whites. As soon as it is all added, but not completely mixed in, stop the machine and remove the bowl.

With a rubber spatula or a large metal spoon, complete mixing in the flour by folding or gently stirring. Stop just as soon as the flour seems blended in.

With a rubber spatula, scrape the batter (9 to 10 cups) into the pan over the almonds and spread evenly. Inscribe a circle deep in the batter to release any large air bubbles.

Bake until no moist patches remain in the surface cracks, the cake springs back when touched, and a cake tester inserted in the center comes out clean, about 50 minutes. Place the pan on a wire rack; *do not turn upside down*. Let cool completely.

Loosen the edges with a knife. Turn the cake out onto a plate (not the rack) and carefully peel off the paper. Put a cake plate over the cake, hold on to both plates, and turn both over together.

Store airtight 1 day at room temperature before serving or freezing. Sift confectioners' sugar over the top before serving.

Apricot Angel Food Cake

12 to 16 Portions.

1½ cups egg whites (see page
xxviii if you need help)

4 ounces dried apricots (1 cup)

1 cup granulated sugar

1 cup all-purpose flour, or 1¼
cups cake flour

1½ teaspoons cream of tartar

1 teaspoon vanilla extract

Confectioners' sugar
(optional)

10 X 4-INCH TUBE PAN OR
9- TO 10-INCH ROUND CAKE PAN
WITH SIDES AT LEAST 3 INCHES
HIGH (A REMOVABLE BOTTOM IS
HELPFUL)

For best flavor, use tart dried apricots from California, not the sweet-to-eat Turkish ones.

Check that one rack is in the middle of the oven and heat the oven to 325°F.

Pour the egg whites into the bowl in which you will be making the batter.

If the pan has a removable bottom, do nothing to it. If it does not, lightly butter the bottom (page xx). Line the bottom with wax paper or parchment paper cut to fit, and lightly butter the paper.

Snip or cut each apricot into 3 or 4 pieces. Finely chop them in a food processor with ¼ cup of the sugar.

Thoroughly mix another ¼ cup of the sugar and the flour in a small bowl. Add the chopped apricots, and toss to mix. Have all the ingredients and tools at hand.

Beat the egg whites with an electric mixer on medium speed for about 2 minutes, until frothy and well broken up. Add the cream of tartar and increase the speed to medium-high. Beat until the whites

lose their yellow cast, greatly increase in volume, and start to turn white.

With the mixer running, slowly sprinkle the remaining ½ cup sugar over the whites. Beat until the whites become very thick, very glossy, and white, and the beaters leave a deep trail. Depending on the mixer, this need take only about 3 minutes total. Beat in the vanilla.

Reduce the speed to the lowest possible. Quickly sprinkle the flour-sugar-apricot mixture over the whites. As soon as it is all added, but not completely mixed in, stop the machine and remove the bowl.

With a rubber spatula or a large metal spoon, complete mixing in the flour by folding or gently stirring. Stop just as soon as the flour seems blended in.

With a rubber spatula, scrape the batter (10 to 10½ cups) into the pan and spread evenly. Inscribe a circle deep in the batter to release any large air bubbles.

Bake until no moist patches remain in the surface cracks, the cake springs back when touched, and a cake tester inserted in the center comes out clean—about 50 minutes for a 10 x 3-inch pan, 1 hour for a tube pan. Turn the pan upside down on a wire rack. Let cool completely.

Loosen the edges (and tube) with a knife. Turn out the cake, loosen and remove the pan bottom, or peel off the paper. Store airtight 1 day at room temperature before serving or freezing. If you wish, sift confectioners' sugar over the top before serving.

Fresh Ginger–Brown Sugar Angel Food Cake

12 to 16 Portions.

1½ cups egg whites (see page xxviii if you need help)
Fresh gingerroot
1¼ cups granulated sugar
1 cup all-purpose flour, or 1¼ cups cake flour
1½ teaspoons cream of tartar
2 tablespoons freshly squeezed lemon juice

¼ cup mild molasses
Confectioners' sugar (optional)

10 X 4-INCH TUBE PAN OR 9- TO 10-INCH ROUND CAKE PAN WITH SIDES AT LEAST 3 INCHES HIGH (A REMOVABLE BOTTOM IS HELPFUL)

Check that one rack is in the middle of the oven and heat the oven to 325°F.

Pour the egg whites into the bowl in which you will be making the batter.

If the pan has a removable bottom, do nothing to it. If it does not, lightly butter the bottom (page xx). Line the bottom with wax paper or parchment paper cut to fit, and lightly butter the paper.

Peel an inch or two of the ginger with a vegetable peeler or knife. Using a rasper or a grater with small V-shapes, grate enough to make 2 tablespoons, lightly pressed down to measure.

Thoroughly mix ¼ cup of the sugar and the flour in a small bowl. Have all the ingredients and tools at hand.

Beat the egg whites with an electric mixer on medium speed for about 2 minutes, until frothy and well broken up. Add the cream of tartar and increase the speed to medium-high. Beat until the whites

lose their yellow cast, greatly increase in volume, and start to turn white.

With the mixer running, slowly sprinkle the remaining 1 cup sugar over the whites. Beat until the whites become very thick, very glossy, and white, and the beaters leave a deep trail. Depending on the mixer, this need take only about 3 minutes total. Beat in the lemon juice and grated ginger.

Reduce the speed to the lowest possible. Pour in the molasses. Beat a few seconds, scraping the sides of the bowl with a rubber spatula to make sure all the molasses is incorporated.

Quickly sprinkle the flour-sugar mixture over the whites. As soon as it is all added, but not completely mixed in, stop the machine and remove the bowl.

With a rubber spatula or a large metal spoon, complete mixing in the flour by folding or gently stirring. Stop just as soon as the flour seems blended in.

With a rubber spatula, scrape the batter (9 cups) into the pan and spread evenly. Inscribe a circle deep in the batter to release any large air bubbles.

Bake until no moist patches remain in the surface cracks, the cake springs back when touched, and a cake tester inserted in the center comes out clean—about 45 minutes for a 10 x 3-inch pan, 50 minutes for a tube pan. Turn the cake pan upside down on a wire rack. Let cool completely.

Loosen the edges (and tube) with a knife. Turn out the cake, loosen and remove the pan bottom, or peel off the paper. Store airtight 1 day at room temperature before serving or freezing. If you wish, sift confectioners' sugar over the top before serving.

Whole White Wheat–Brown Sugar Angel Food Cake

12 to 16 Portions

1½ cups egg whites (see page xxviii if you need help)

1¼ cups granulated sugar

1 cup whole-white-wheat flour

1½ teaspoons cream of tartar

1 teaspoon ground cinnamon

1 teaspoon vanilla extract

¼ cup mild or dark molasses

Confectioners' sugar (optional)

10 x 4-INCH TUBE PAN OR 9- TO 10-INCH ROUND CAKE PAN WITH SIDES AT LEAST 3 INCHES HIGH (A REMOVABLE BOTTOM IS HELPFUL)

Whole-white-wheat flour is just beginning to be widely available, but it is worth searching out because white wheat leaves none of that bitter aftertaste that regular (red) whole wheat does. Try this cake with Superb Chocolate Sauce (page 166), Nutmeg-Honey Whipped Cream (page 161), or Caramel Apples (page 165).

Check that one rack is in the middle of the oven and heat the oven to 325°F.

Pour the egg whites into the bowl in which you will be making the batter.

If the pan has a removable bottom, do nothing to it. If it does not, lightly butter the bottom (page xx). Line the bottom with wax paper or parchment paper cut to fit, and lightly butter the paper.

Thoroughly mix ¼ cup of the sugar and the flour in a small bowl. Have all the ingredients and tools at hand.

Beat the egg whites with an electric mixer on medium speed for about 2 minutes, until frothy and well broken up. Add the cream of tartar and increase the speed to medium-high. Beat until the whites lose their yellow cast, greatly increase in volume, and start to turn white.

With the mixer running, slowly sprinkle the remaining 1 cup sugar over the whites. Add the cinnamon and vanilla. Beat until the whites become very thick, very glossy, and white, and the beaters leave a deep trail. Depending on the mixer, this need take only about 3 minutes total.

Reduce the speed to the lowest possible. Pour in the molasses. Beat a few seconds, scraping the sides of the bowl with a rubber spatula to make sure all the molasses is incorporated.

Quickly sprinkle the flour-sugar mixture over the whites. As soon as it is all added, but not completely mixed in, stop the machine and remove the bowl.

With a rubber spatula or a large metal spoon, complete mixing in the flour by folding or gently stirring. Stop just as soon as the flour seems blended in.

With a rubber spatula, scrape the batter (9 cups) into the pan and spread evenly. Inscribe a circle deep in the batter to release any large air bubbles.

Bake until no moist patches remain in the surface cracks, the cake springs back when touched, and a cake tester inserted in the center comes out clean—about 50 minutes for a 10 x 3-inch pan, 1 hour for a tube pan. Turn the pan upside down on a wire rack. Let cool completely.

Loosen the edges (and tube) with a knife. Turn out the cake, loosen and remove the pan bottom, or peel off the paper. Store airtight 1 day at room temperature before serving or freezing. If you wish, sift confectioners' sugar over the top before serving.

Lemon-Vanilla Angel Food Cake

12 to 16 Portions

1½ cups egg whites (see page
   xxviii if you need help)
1 cup all-purpose flour, or 1¼
   cups cake flour
1 cup granulated sugar, or 2
   cups confectioners' sugar
1½ teaspoons cream of tartar
3 tablespoons freshly squeezed
   lemon juice

1 teaspoon vanilla extract
Confectioners' sugar
   (optional)
10 x 4-INCH TUBE PAN OR
9- TO 10-INCH ROUND CAKE PAN
WITH SIDES AT LEAST 3 INCHES
HIGH (A REMOVABLE BOTTOM IS
HELPFUL)

Excellent with Raspberry-Blueberry Sauce (page 163) or a scoop of lemon or lime sorbet, or one of the wilder sorbets such as passion fruit. For a classy dessert, lay a slender wedge of the cake flat on each plate, place tiny scoops of 2 or 3 sorbets alongside, and decorate with a chocolate twig candy. Sift a little confectioners' sugar over all, including the plate.

Check that one rack is in the middle of the oven and heat the oven to 325°F.

Pour the egg whites into the bowl in which you will be making the batter.

If the pan has a removable bottom, do nothing to it. If it does not, lightly butter the bottom (page xx). Line the bottom with wax paper or parchment paper cut to fit, and lightly butter the paper.

Thoroughly mix the flour and ¼ cup of the granulated sugar or ½ cup of the confectioners' sugar in a small bowl. Have all the ingredients and tools at hand.

Beat the egg whites with an electric mixer on medium speed for about 2 minutes, until frothy and well broken up. Add the cream of tartar and increase the speed to medium-high. Beat until the whites lose their yellow cast, greatly increase in volume, and start to turn white.

With the mixer running, slowly sprinkle the remaining ¾ cup sugar over the whites. Beat until the whites become very thick, very glossy, and white, and the beaters leave a deep trail. Depending on the mixer, this need take only about 3 minutes total. Beat in the lemon juice and vanilla, just enough to mix.

Reduce the speed to the lowest possible. Quickly sprinkle the flour-sugar mixture over the whites. As soon as it is all added, but not completely mixed in, stop the machine and remove the bowl.

With a rubber spatula or a large metal spoon, complete mixing in the flour by folding or gently stirring. Stop just as soon as the flour seems blended in.

With a rubber spatula, scrape the batter (9 cups) into the pan and spread evenly. Inscribe a circle deep in the batter to release any large air bubbles.

Bake until no moist patches remain in the surface cracks, the cake springs back when touched, and a cake tester inserted in the center comes out clean—about 50 minutes for a 10 x 3-inch pan, 1 hour for a tube pan. Turn the pan upside down on a wire rack. Let cool completely.

Loosen the edges (and tube) with a knife. Turn out the cake, loosen and remove the pan bottom, or peel off the paper. Store airtight 1 day at room temperature before serving or freezing. If you wish, sift confectioners' sugar over the top before serving.

Hazelnut-Chocolate Angel Food Cake

12 to 16 Portions

1½ cups egg whites (see page xxviii if you need help)
½ cup toasted chopped hazelnuts (page xxv)
1¾ cups granulated sugar
⅔ cup all-purpose flour
⅔ cup unsweetened cocoa powder
1½ teaspoons cream of tartar
1 tablespoon vanilla extract
Confectioners' sugar
9- TO 10-INCH ROUND CAKE PAN WITH SIDES AT LEAST 3 INCHES HIGH (A REMOVABLE BOTTOM IS HELPFUL)

The combination of hazelnut and chocolate is close to the top of my favorite-flavor chart, but it's hard to achieve in an angel food cake because the oil in nuts causes the beaten egg whites to collapse. The same problem arose with the Caramel-Coffee Angel Food Cake on page 84. The surprisingly simple solution is to sprinkle the nuts on the bottom of the pan, where they form a wonderful toasty crust. True, this makes neat slices a problem, but the flavor is worth it. Put the cake nut-side down on the serving plate, then sprinkle the surface with confectioners' sugar. Cut straight through the nuts with a sharp knife. Because of the lavish amount of cocoa, the cake itself is more like a dense mousse and only about 1½ inches high. Toasted almonds, pecans, or walnuts can be used instead of the hazelnuts.

Check that one rack is in the middle of the oven and heat the oven to 325°F.

Pour the egg whites into the bowl in which you will be making the batter.

Lightly butter the bottom of the pan (page xx). Line the bottom with wax paper or parchment paper cut to fit, and lightly butter the paper. Sprinkle the toasted chopped hazelnuts evenly over the bottom of the pan.

Thoroughly mix ½ cup of the sugar, the flour, and the cocoa in a small bowl. Have all the ingredients and tools at hand.

Beat the egg whites with an electric mixer on medium speed for about 2 minutes, until frothy and well broken up. Add the cream of tartar and increase the speed to medium-high. Beat until the whites lose their yellow cast, greatly increase in volume, and start to turn white.

With the mixer running, slowly sprinkle the remaining 1¼ cups sugar over the whites. Beat until the whites become very thick, very glossy, and white, and the beaters leave a deep trail. Depending on the mixer, this need take only about 3 minutes total. Add the vanilla.

Reduce the speed to the lowest possible. Quickly sprinkle the flour-cocoa mixture over the whites. As soon as it is all added, but not completely mixed in, stop the machine and remove the bowl.

With a rubber spatula or a large metal spoon, complete mixing in the flour by folding or gently stirring. Stop just as soon as the flour seems blended in.

With a rubber spatula, scrape the batter (8 cups) into the pan over the hazelnuts and spread evenly. Inscribe a circle deep in the batter to release any large air bubbles.

Bake until no moist patches remain in the surface cracks, the cake springs back when touched, and a cake tester inserted in the center comes out clean, about 50 minutes. Place the pan on a wire rack; *do not turn upside down*. Let cool completely.

Loosen the edges with a knife. Turn the cake out onto the rack and carefully peel off the paper. Put a cake plate over the cake, hold on to the rack and plate, and turn both over together. Store airtight 1 day at room temperature before serving or freezing. Sift confectioners' sugar over the top before serving.

Cappuccino Angel Food Cake

12 to 16 Portions

1½ cups egg whites (see page xxviii if you need help)

1 cup plus 2 tablespoons granulated sugar

1 cup all-purpose flour, or 1¼ cups cake flour

1 teaspoon ground cinnamon

1½ teaspoons cream of tartar

1 tablespoon instant coffee powder or granules, preferably espresso

9- TO 10-INCH ROUND CAKE PAN WITH SIDES AT LEAST 3 INCHES HIGH OR 10 X 4-INCH TUBE PAN (A REMOVABLE BOTTOM IS HELPFUL)

Every bite or two you get a tiny crunchy jolt of cinnamon sugar. If you wish, sift 1 tablespoon cocoa or 1 teaspoon cinnamon and 1 tablespoon confectioners' sugar over the cake just before serving.

Check that one rack is in the middle of the oven and heat the oven to 325°F.

Pour the egg whites into the bowl in which you will be making the batter.

If the pan has a removable bottom, do nothing to it. If it does not, lightly butter the bottom (page xx). Line the bottom with wax paper or parchment paper cut to fit, and lightly butter the paper.

Thoroughly mix ¼ cup of the sugar and the flour in a small bowl. Mix the 2 tablespoons sugar and the cinnamon in a small dish. Have all the ingredients and tools at hand.

Beat the egg whites with an electric mixer on medium speed for about 2 minutes, until frothy and well broken up. Add the cream of tartar and increase the speed to medium-high. Beat until the whites lose their yellow cast, greatly increase in volume, and start to turn white.

With the mixer running, slowly sprinkle the remaining ¾ cup sugar over the whites. After 3 or 4 tablespoons, add the coffee powder. Beat until the whites become very thick, very glossy, and pale beige, and the beaters leave a deep trail. Depending on the mixer, this need take only about 3 minutes total.

Reduce the speed to the lowest possible. Quickly sprinkle the flour-sugar mixture over the whites. As soon as it is all added, but not completely mixed in, stop the machine and remove the bowl.

With a rubber spatula or a large metal spoon, complete mixing in the flour by folding or gently stirring. Stop just as soon as the flour seems blended in.

With a rubber spatula, scrape about half the 8 to 9 cups batter in the pan and spread evenly. Sprinkle the cinnamon sugar evenly over the surface. Drop spoonfuls of the remaining batter over the cinnamon sugar and spread fairly evenly. Using the spatula, inscribe a circle deep in the batter to release any large air bubbles.

Bake until no moist patches remain in the surface cracks, the cake springs back when touched, and a cake tester inserted in the center comes out clean, about 50 minutes.

Turn the pan upside down on a wire rack. Let cool completely.

Loosen the edges (and tube) with a knife. Turn out the cake, loosen and remove the pan bottom, or peel off the paper. Store airtight 1 day at room temperature before serving or freezing.

Peppermint Stick Angel Food Cake

12 to 16 Portions

1½ cups egg whites (see page xxviii if you need help)

About 14 round red-and-white peppermint candies

1¼ cups cake flour, or 1 cup all-purpose flour

2½ cups confectioners' sugar, or 1 cup granulated sugar

1½ teaspoons cream of tartar

1 teaspoon vanilla extract

Confectioners' sugar (optional)

10 x 4-INCH TUBE PAN OR 9- TO 10-INCH ROUND CAKE PAN WITH SIDES AT LEAST 3 INCHES HIGH (A REMOVABLE BOTTOM IS HELPFUL)

If you love peppermint stick ice cream, you'll love this cake. And if you love mint chocolate chip ice cream even more, try the recipe that follows. A small scoop of ice cream—vanilla or, what the heck, peppermint stick—and/or a spoonful of chocolate sauce make a wedge of either cake into a spectacular dessert.

Check that one rack is in the middle of the oven and heat the oven to 325°F.

Pour the egg whites into the bowl in which you will be making the batter.

If the pan has a removable bottom, do nothing to it. If it does not, lightly butter the bottom (page xx). Line the bottom with wax paper or parchment paper cut to fit, and lightly butter the paper.

Finely chop the mints in a food processor, or, a few at a time, in a blender. You need ¼ cup.

Thoroughly mix the flour and ½ cup of the confectioners' sugar or ¼ cup granulated sugar in a bowl. Have all the ingredients and tools at hand.

Beat the egg whites with an electric mixer on medium speed for about 2 minutes, until frothy and well broken up. Add the cream of tartar and increase the speed to medium-high. Beat until the whites lose their yellow cast, greatly increase in volume, and start to turn white.

With the mixer running, slowly sprinkle the remaining sugar over the whites. Beat until the whites become very thick, very glossy, and white, and the beaters leave a deep trail. Depending on the mixer, this need take only about 3 minutes total. Add the crushed peppermint candy and the vanilla; beat just enough to mix.

Reduce the speed to the lowest possible. Quickly sprinkle the flour-sugar mixture over the whites. As soon as it is all added, but not completely mixed in, stop the machine and remove the bowl. With a rubber spatula or a large metal spoon, complete mixing in the flour by folding or gently stirring. Stop just as soon as the flour seems blended in.

With a rubber spatula, scrape the batter (9 cups) into the pan and spread evenly. Inscribe a circle deep in the batter to release any large air bubbles.

Bake until no moist patches remain in the surface cracks, the cake is light brown and springs back when touched, and a cake tester inserted in the center comes out clean—about 50 minutes for a 10 x 3-inch pan, 1 hour for a tube pan. Turn the pan upside down on a wire rack. Let cool completely.

Loosen the edges (and tube) with a knife. Remove the pan, loosen and remove the pan bottom, or peel off the paper. Store airtight at room temperature at least 1 day before serving or freezing. If you wish, sift confectioners' sugar over the cake before serving.

Chocolate-Mint Angel Food Cake

Use the same ingredients and pan as for Peppermint Stick Angel Food Cake (page 98), plus: 2 ounces bittersweet or semisweet chocolate, finely chopped.

You can chop the chocolate by hand, in a food processor, or about one-third at a time in a blender.

Follow directions for the Peppermint Stick Angel Food Cake, tossing in the chopped chocolate with the flour-sugar mixture. Proceed and bake as directed.

Rich and smooth, with a fine crumb, pound cakes have a sweet, buttery flavor that comes from lots of butter and sugar. They keep especially well, so why not make two while you have the ingredients out and stash one in your freezer? A good recipe to start with is Miriam's Sour Cream Pound Cake, page 108.

Pound Cakes

Pound cakes get their name from old recipes that call for a pound each of butter, sugar, and flour. You can vary those proportions considerably and still end up with a cake that has the distinctive sweet, buttery smell and moist, fine texture of a pound cake. (Compared to, say, the more open texture of a coffeecake, which is a shade closer to bread.) A good pound cake has no large holes in it and crumbles when rubbed between your fingers. Pound cakes are made by beating butter and sugar to incorporate air, beating in eggs, and adding the flour by hand with a wooden spoon or with a mixer on low. While many pound cakes rely totally on the air beaten in to make them rise, I do like to include a small amount of baking powder for insurance.

Here's the plan of action for making a pound cake:
- Check that you have all the ingredients.
- Bring the eggs and the butter to room temperature.
- Turn on the oven.
- Prepare the pan.
- Prepare all other ingredients.
- Make the batter and bake it.

Because of the high proportion of fat in a pound cake, the pan needs only a very light greasing. I prefer to use butter, but vegetable shortening or cooking spray works fine, too.

When *butter* for pound cake is "at room temperature," it is soft enough to beat easily, but not so soft that it is practically melted. Depending on the time available and the temperature of your kitchen you might:
- Leave the butter in its wrapper on the counter for an hour or so.
- Open the butter wrapper and cut as much as you need into small pieces. Leave at room temperature 30 minutes to 1 hour.
- Put the unwrapped butter in a small microwave-safe dish.

Microwave in 10-second increments, poking the butter to test it after each 10-second interval, until it is soft. Be very careful! If you melt the butter, start again. Melted butter will not beat up light and fluffy with the sugar.

Eggs for pound cake should be at room temperature, too, to help prevent the butter and sugar mixture from "breaking" or "curdling," that is, breaking into small particles. (If that happens, don't worry about it. You will lose some volume, but it is not a disaster.) To warm eggs quickly, put them, in their shells, in a bowl of very warm water. After 5 minutes or so, pour off the cooled water and add fresh warm water. After 5 to 10 minutes longer, the eggs will be ready to use. Another way is to break all the eggs into a bowl and beat them with a fork. Let them stand 10 to 15 minutes at room temperature, then add them to the mixture about ¼ cup at a time (don't measure, just guess).

Pound cakes can be eaten freshly baked, once they have cooled. But for best flavor, tightly wrap the cooled cake (or put in an airtight container), and let stand 1 day at room temperature for the flavor to develop.

Sour Cream and Walnut Spice Cake

12 Portions

1¼ teaspoons ground nutmeg

1 teaspoon ground cinnamon

½ teaspoon ground allspice

¼ teaspoon ground cardamom

1 cup plus 4 tablespoons granulated sugar

14 tablespoons (1¾ sticks) unsalted butter, at room temperature

2 teaspoons vanilla extract

4 large eggs, at room temperature

¾ cup sour cream

1 teaspoon baking powder

¼ teaspoon baking soda

¼ teaspoon salt

1 cup chopped walnuts

2¼ cups all-purpose flour

9 x 5 x 3-INCH LOAF PAN

Heat the oven to 325°F. Grease the pan and line with foil, letting it hang over the sides. Grease the foil.

Mix the spices in a cup. Mix ¼ teaspoon of the spice mixture with 2 tablespoons of the sugar, and set aside to use for the topping.

Beat the butter, the remaining 1 cup plus 2 tablespoons sugar, and the vanilla with an electric mixer on high speed, until pale and fluffy.

Reduce the speed to medium. Add the eggs, one at a time, beating after each.

Reduce the mixer speed to low. Stir in the sour cream, the remaining spice mixture, the baking powder, baking soda, and salt. Add the walnuts. Scrape the sides of the bowl often.

With the mixer still on low, stir in the flour just until incorporated. Do not overmix.

Spread the batter (6 cups) in the prepared pan. Sprinkle the reserved sugar-spice mixture over the top. (It will look like too much topping, but it isn't.)

Bake until a cake tester inserted in the center comes out clean, about 1 hour and 10 minutes.

Cool the cake in the pan on a wire rack for about 30 minutes. Lift the cake from the pan by the foil. Let cool completely on the wire rack. Remove the foil. For best flavor, wrap airtight, being careful not to disturb the sugar topping too much, and store 1 day at room temperature before serving or freezing.

Sour Cream–Chocolate Chip Pound Cake

12 Portions

1 cup plus 4 tablespoons granulated sugar

1½ teaspoons ground
cinnamon

14 tablespoons (1¾ sticks)
unsalted butter,
at room temperature

2 teaspoons vanilla extract

4 large eggs, at room temperature

¾ cup sour cream

1 teaspoon baking powder

¼ teaspoon baking soda

¼ teaspoon salt

2¼ cups all-purpose flour

1½ cups semisweet chocolate
chips

9 x 5 x 3-INCH LOAF PAN

Heat the oven to 325°F. Grease the pan and line with foil, letting it hang over the sides. Grease the foil.

Mix 2 tablespoons of the sugar with ¼ teaspoon of the cinnamon, and set aside to use for the topping.

Beat the butter, the remaining 1 cup plus 2 tablespoons sugar, and the vanilla with an electric mixer on high speed, until pale and fluffy.

Reduce the speed to medium. Add the eggs, one at a time, beating after each.

Beat in the sour cream, baking powder, baking soda, salt, and the remaining 1¼ teaspoons cinnamon. Scrape the sides of the bowl often.

With the mixer on low, stir in the flour until nearly incorporated. Add the chocolate chips and stir until the batter is well mixed.

Spread the batter (6½ cups) in the pan (the pan will be very full). Sprinkle the reserved cinnamon sugar over the top. (It will look like too much topping, but it isn't.)

Bake until a cake tester inserted in the center comes out clean, about 1 hour and 10 minutes.

Cool the cake in the pan on a wire rack for about 30 minutes. Lift the cake from the pan by the foil. Let cool completely on the wire rack. Remove the foil. For best flavor, wrap airtight, being careful not to disturb the sugar topping more than necessary, and store 1 day at room temperature before serving or freezing.

Miriam's Sour Cream Pound Cake

12 Portions

1 cup plus 2 tablespoons
   granulated sugar, or 2 cups
   confectioners' sugar
14 tablespoons (1¾ sticks)
   unsalted butter,
   at room temperature
1 tablespoon vanilla extract
4 large eggs, at room temperature

¾ cup sour cream
1 teaspoon baking powder
¼ teaspoon baking soda
¼ teaspoon salt
2¼ cups all-purpose flour, or
   2½ cups cake flour
2 tablespoons granulated
   sugar, for topping
9 x 5 x 3-INCH LOAF PAN

Miriam Rubin has a flair for food and flavor that I admit to envying. Now a food writer and editor, she was the first woman chef at the Four Seasons restaurant in New York City.

Heat the oven to 325°F. Grease the pan and line with foil, letting it hang over the sides. Grease the foil.

Beat the sugar, butter, and vanilla with an electric mixer on high speed, until pale and fluffy.

Reduce the speed to medium. Add the eggs, one at a time, beating after each.

Beat in the sour cream, baking powder, baking soda, and salt. Scrape the sides of the bowl often.

With the mixer on low, stir in the flour just until incorporated. Do not overmix.

Spread the batter (5 cups) in the pan. Sprinkle the 2 tablespoons granulated sugar for the topping over the top. (It will look like too much sugar, but it isn't.)

Bake until a cake tester inserted in the center comes out clean, about 1 hour and 10 minutes.

Cool the cake in the pan on a wire rack for about 30 minutes. Lift the cake from the pan by the foil. Let cool completely on the wire rack. Remove the foil. For best flavor, wrap airtight, being careful not to disturb the sugar topping too much, and store 1 day at room temperature before serving or freezing.

Hazelnut Pound Cake

12 Portions.

1 cup toasted hazelnuts (page xxvii; see Note)

1 cup granulated sugar

16 tablespoons (2 sticks) unsalted butter, at room temperature

1 teaspoon vanilla extract

4 large eggs, at room temperature

1 teaspoon baking powder

¼ teaspoon salt

2 cups all-purpose flour, or 2¼ cups cake flour

9 x 5 x 3-INCH LOAF PAN

Fantastic flavor that improves with time. Good with tea, coffee, or a glass of sherry or dessert wine. Try the easy food processor method, but be sure to use a machine with a full-size (8 cups or larger) work bowl.

Heat the oven to 325°F. Grease the pan.

Food processor method: Process the hazelnuts and sugar until the nuts are finely chopped, about 30 seconds. Add the butter and vanilla and process about 30 seconds, until pale and creamy.

With the machine still running, add the eggs, one at a time. Add the baking powder and salt. Scrape the sides of the bowl. Sprinkle the flour over the surface. Turn the machine on/off several times, until the mixture is smooth and well blended.

Spread the batter (4 to 5 cups) evenly in the pan. Bake until a cake tester inserted in the center comes out clean, about 1 hour and 20 to 25 minutes.

Cool the cake in the pan on a wire rack for about 30 minutes.

Loosen the edges and turn the cake out. Let cool completely. Store airtight at least 1 day at room temperature before serving or freezing.

Electric mixer method: Grind the toasted hazelnuts in a nut mill or in batches in a blender, or chop as fine as possible with a knife. Beat the sugar and butter in a large bowl with an electric mixer on high speed about 5 minutes, until pale and fluffy. Reduce the speed to medium. Add the eggs, one at a time, beating after each. Scrape the sides of the bowl often.

Add the hazelnuts, baking powder, salt, and vanilla. Beat to blend well. With the mixer on low, add the flour and mix only until just incorporated. Do not overmix. Bake and store as above.

NOTE: If you can buy hazelnuts already toasted and chopped, simply process them briefly with the sugar.

Caraway Seed Cake

12 Portions.

2 tablespoons caraway seeds
1 cup granulated sugar
16 tablespoons (2 sticks)
  unsalted butter,
  at room temperature
4 large eggs, at room temperature

1 teaspoon baking powder
¼ teaspoon salt
2 cups all-purpose flour, or 2¼
  cups cake flour
9 x 5 x 3-INCH OR
8½ x 4½ x 2¾-INCH LOAF PAN

One of my favorites.
Heat the oven to 325°F. Grease the pan.

Food processor method: Process the caraway seeds and the sugar for 1 to 2 minutes. Let the sugar dust settle before you open the container. The seeds won't turn to powder, but processing does help release the flavor. Add the butter and process about 30 seconds, until pale and creamy.

With the machine still running, add the eggs, one at a time. Add the baking powder and salt. Scrape the sides of the bowl. Sprinkle the flour over the surface. Turn the machine on/off several times, until the mixture is smooth and well blended.

Spread the batter (3 to 4 cups) evenly in the pan. Bake until a cake tester inserted in the center comes out clean—about 1 hour and 10 to 15 minutes for the larger pan, close to 1½ hours for the smaller pan.

Cool the cake in the pan on a wire rack for about 30 minutes. Loosen the edges and turn the cake out. Let cool completely. Store airtight 1 to 2 days at room temperature before serving or freezing.

Electric mixer method: Grind the seeds in a nut mill and add with the sugar. Or, put ½ cup of the sugar in a blender and sprinkle the seeds on top of the sugar. Blend or grind for 30 to 60 seconds (seeds will break up). Allow the sugar dust to settle before you open the container. Beat the butter and all of the sugar in a large bowl with an electric mixer on high speed about 5 minutes, until pale and fluffy. Reduce the speed to medium. Add the eggs, one at a time, beating after each. Scrape the sides of the bowl often. Add the baking powder and salt. Beat to blend well. With the mixer on low, add the flour and mix only until just incorporated. Do not overmix. Bake and store as above.

Tennessee Whiskey Cake

12 Portions

1¼ cups pecans plus 10 to 16 pecan halves for decoration

16 tablespoons (2 sticks) unsalted butter, at room temperature

¾ cup granulated sugar

½ cup packed dark brown sugar

2 teaspoons vanilla extract

5 large eggs, at room temperature

¼ cup sour-mash whiskey or bourbon

1 teaspoon baking powder

¼ teaspoon baking soda

¼ teaspoon salt

2 cups all-purpose flour, or 2¼ cups cake flour

9 x 3-INCH SPRINGFORM PAN, OR

9 x 5 x 3-INCH LOAF PAN, OR

10-CUP TUBE PAN

This keeps real well in the refrigerator or freezer. Serve thin slices with a small scoop of ice cream or Nutmeg-Honey Whipped Cream (page 161).

Heat the oven to 400°F. Spread the 1¼ cups pecans on a baking sheet and bake 10 to 15 minutes, stirring occasionally, until toasted and lightly browned. Cool. Grind about half the nuts in a food processor. Add the rest of the toasted nuts and turn the machine on/off three or four times to chop coarsely.

Meanwhile, reduce the oven temperature to 325°F. and grease the pan.

Beat the butter, sugars, and vanilla with an electric mixer on high speed, until light and fluffy.

Reduce the speed to medium. Add the eggs, one at a time, beating after each.

Beat in the whiskey or bourbon, the baking powder, baking soda, and salt (the batter will look curdled). Stir in the chopped pecans.

With the mixer on low, stir in the flour until just incorporated. Do not overmix.

Spread the batter (6 cups) in the prepared pan. Smooth the top with a spatula. Arrange the pecan halves on top of the batter.

Bake until a cake tester inserted in the center comes out clean and the cake is springy to the touch and shrinks from the sides of the pan, about 50 minutes to 1 hour.

Cool the cake in the pan on a wire rack for about 30 minutes. Loosen the edges. Turn the cake out or remove the sides of the springform pan, and with a thin metal spatula, slide the cake off the metal pan bottom to a wire rack. Let cool completely. For best flavor, store airtight 1 day at room temperature before serving or freezing.

Triple-Ginger Pound Cake

12 Portions

3 to 4 ounces fresh gingerroot

2 to 3 ounces crystallized ginger

1 cup granulated sugar

16 tablespoons (2 sticks)
unsalted butter,
at room temperature

4 large eggs, at room temperature

1 teaspoon baking powder

½ teaspoon ground ginger

¼ teaspoon salt

2 cups all-purpose flour

9 x 5 x 3-INCH LOAF PAN

Each kind of ginger contributes its own special quality to this wonderful mellow cake, studded with flecks of crystallized ginger. Buy
crystallized ginger by the pound at candy shops or some specialty
food shops. It's much less expensive than buying tiny jars from the
supermarket spice section.

Heat the oven to 325°F. Grease the pan.

Peel the fresh ginger with a knife or vegetable peeler and coarsely
chop enough to make ¼ cup.

Reserve a few pieces of the crystallized ginger to decorate the top
of the cake. Put the fresh ginger and the remaining crystallized ginger
in a food processor, along with the sugar. Process 3 to 4 minutes to
grind the gingers finely. The sugar will get quite damp.

Add the butter and process about 1 minute, until the mixture is
pale and fluffy. With the machine still running, add the eggs, one at a
time, stopping the machine once to scrape the sides of the bowl.

Add the baking powder, ground ginger, and salt. Process briefly to mix. Scrape the sides of the bowl. Sprinkle the flour over the surface. Turn the machine on/off several times, just until the flour is blended, scraping the sides of the bowl once.

Spread the batter (4 to 5 cups) in the pan. Draw the handle of a rubber spatula once lengthwise through the batter ½ inch deep. (This will bake into an attractive split.)

Slice the reserved crystallized ginger thin, and scatter or arrange on top of the batter. Bake until a cake tester inserted in the center comes out clean, about 1 hour and 25 minutes.

Cool the cake in the pan on a wire rack for 30 to 40 minutes. Loosen the edges and turn out the cake. Let cool completely. Store airtight 1 day at room temperature before serving or freezing.

Walnut–Poppy Seed Pound Cake

16 Portions

½ cup poppy seeds (3 ounces)
1 cup granulated sugar
1 cup walnuts
16 tablespoons (2 sticks)
  unsalted butter,
  at room temperature

4 large eggs,
  at room temperature
1 teaspoon baking powder
1 teaspoon vanilla extract
¼ teaspoon salt
2 cups all-purpose flour

9 x 5 x 3-INCH LOAF PAN

The inspiration for this cake was one created by Ilse Loipner, when she was pastry chef at Windows on the World restaurant in New York City. This delicate, beautiful cake is perfect for any occasion, with a glass of dessert wine, French roast coffee, or Earl Grey tea. Try to buy good, fresh poppy seeds from a source with a fast turnover. A store selling Middle European or Middle Eastern groceries is a much better bet (and usually much less expensive) than the little jars or boxes sold in the supermarket spice section, which may have lingered there for years. If you're in a hurry, you can omit toasting the seeds and nuts.

Blender and electric mixer method: "Grind" the poppy seeds in a blender for 2 minutes. The seeds will darken but will not turn to powder or paste. Add about ¼ cup of the sugar and "grind" about 1 minute longer. Do not remove the blender lid until the cloud of sugar has settled.

Put a plate or a sheet of foil next to the stove top. Tip the poppy seed mixture into a heavy skillet, 8 to 9 inches across the bottom. Grind the walnuts in two batches in the blender, and add to the skillet. Stir over moderate heat for 6 to 7 minutes, until the seeds and nuts smell toasted. Scrape the hot mixture onto the plate or sheet of foil so it stops cooking. Spread it out and let cool completely. (If the mixture is warm it may melt the butter and a very dense, although still delicious, cake will result.) Set aside about 2 tablespoons of the poppy seed mixture to sprinkle on top of the cake. (This much can be done a day or so ahead; refrigerate the cooled mixture in an airtight container.)

Meanwhile, heat the oven to 325°F. and grease the pan.

Beat the butter and the remaining ¾ cup sugar with an electric mixer on high speed, until pale and fluffy. Add two of the eggs, one at a time, beating after each. Beat in about half the remaining poppy seed mixture. Beat in the remaining eggs, then the remaining poppy seed mixture. Beat in the baking powder, vanilla, and salt.

With the mixer on low, add the flour. Stir just until incorporated. Do not overmix.

Spread the batter (4 to 5 cups) evenly in the pan. Sprinkle with the reserved 2 tablespoons poppy seed mixture. Bake until a cake tester inserted in the center comes out clean, about 1 hour and 5 to 15 minutes.

Cool the cake in the pan on a wire rack for about 30 minutes. Loosen the edges and turn the cake out. Let cool completely. Serve freshly baked, or wrap airtight and store up to 5 days at room temperature or freeze.

Food processor method: Process the poppy seeds, ¼ cup of the sugar, and the walnuts in a food processor in the same way as for the blender, then toast in the skillet and cool completely. Process the butter and the remaining ¾ cup sugar for 1 or 2 minutes, until pale and fluffy. With the machine running, add the eggs, one at a time. Add the baking powder, vanilla, and salt. Process to mix. Reserve 2 tablespoons of the poppy seed mixture for the topping. Add the remaining poppy seed mixture and process briefly to mix. Sprinkle the flour over the surface. Process a few seconds, just to incorporate, scraping the sides of bowl once. Bake and store as directed.

Soaked Orange Pound Cake

12 Portions

CAKE

2 medium-size navel oranges

1 cup granulated sugar, or
  2 cups confectioners' sugar

16 tablespoons (2 sticks)
  unsalted butter,
  at room temperature

1½ teaspoons vanilla extract

4 large eggs, at room temperature

1 teaspoon baking powder

¼ teaspoon salt

2 cups all-purpose flour, or 2¼
  cups cake flour

SYRUP

⅓ cup freshly squeezed orange
  juice (use oranges from cake
  plus additional juice, if
  needed)

3 tablespoons granulated
  sugar

2 teaspoons freshly squeezed
  lemon juice

8- TO 12-CUP TUBE OR BUNDT PAN

Good with a small glass of orange-flavored liqueur or with lemon-ade on the porch on a hot summer afternoon.

Heat the oven to 325°F. Grease the pan well.

Scrub and dry the oranges. With a vegetable peeler, remove the brightly colored part of the peel and measure it. You need ⅓ cup packed. Squeeze the oranges and reserve the juice for the syrup.

Put the orange peel and the sugar in a food processor and process until the peel is very finely chopped. (Instead of using a food processor, you may grate the unpeeled orange and add the peel to the sugar in the bowl.) The sugar will be very damp. Scrape the sugar mixture into the bowl in which you plan to make the batter.

Add the butter and vanilla and beat with an electric mixer on high speed, until pale and fluffy.

Reduce the speed to medium. Add the eggs, one at a time, beating after each. Beat in the baking powder and salt. Scrape the sides of the bowl often.

With the mixer on low, sprinkle in the flour and stir just until incorporated. Do not overmix.

Spread the batter (6 cups) evenly in the pan. Bake until a cake tester inserted in the center comes out clean, about 55 minutes to 1 hour and 5 minutes.

Meanwhile, mix the syrup ingredients in a small saucepan, and stir over moderately high heat until the sugar is dissolved and the syrup is hot. Remove from the heat.

Cool the cake in the pan on a wire rack for 10 minutes. Poke about 36 holes in the cake with a long bamboo or metal skewer. Brush the cake with all but about 1 tablespoon of the warm syrup. The surface will look quite wet. Let stand 10 to 15 minutes. Loosen the edges and turn the cake out. Let cool completely. Brush with the remaining 1 tablespoon orange syrup. For best flavor, store airtight 1 day at room temperature before serving or freezing.

Orange–Chocolate Chunk Pound Cake

12 Portions

3¼ to 4 ounces bittersweet or semisweet chocolate

2 medium-size navel oranges

1 cup granulated sugar

16 tablespoons (2 sticks) unsalted butter, at room temperature

1½ teaspoons vanilla extract

4 large eggs, at room temperature

1 teaspoon baking powder

¼ teaspoon salt

2 cups all-purpose flour, or 2¼ cups cake flour

8- TO 12-CUP TUBE OR BUNDT PAN

Heat the oven to 325°F. Grease the pan well.

Coarsely chop the chocolate with a knife or in a food processor. Scrub and dry 1 orange. With a vegetable peeler, remove the brightly colored part of the peel.

Squeeze the oranges and measure the juice. Add a little water or additional orange juice if needed to bring it up to ⅓ cup.

Put the orange peel and the sugar in a food processor and process until the peel is very finely chopped. (Instead of using a food processor, you may grate the unpeeled orange and add the peel to the sugar in the bowl.) The sugar will be damp. Scrape the sugar mixture into the bowl in which you will make the batter.

Add the butter and vanilla and beat with an electric mixer on high speed, until pale and fluffy.

Reduce the speed to medium. Add the eggs, one at a time, beating after each. Beat in the chopped chocolate, the baking powder, and salt. Scrape the sides of the bowl often.

With the mixer on low, mix in the orange juice. Sprinkle in the flour. Stir just until incorporated. Do not overmix.

Spread the batter (5 cups) evenly in the pan. Bake about 1 hour and 5 minutes. This cake is a little tricky to test for doneness because the cake tester usually comes up covered with hot melted chocolate. Remove the cake from the oven once a cake tester shows that it is *still just slightly damp inside.*

Cool the cake in the pan on a wire rack for 30 to 40 minutes. Loosen the edges and turn the cake out. For best flavor, store airtight 1 day at room temperature before serving or freezing.

Pumpkin Pound Cake

12 Portions

15 tablespoons (2 sticks minus 1 tablespoon) unsalted butter, at room temperature

½ cup granulated sugar, or 1 cup confectioners' sugar

½ cup packed light brown sugar

2 teaspoons vanilla extract

4 large eggs, at room temperature

2⅓ cups all-purpose flour, or 2⅔ cups cake flour

1 teaspoon baking powder

1 teaspoon ground cinnamon

1 teaspoon ground nutmeg

½ teaspoon ground ginger

¼ teaspoon baking soda

¼ teaspoon salt

¼ teaspoon ground cloves

1 cup canned plain pumpkin (half a 16-ounce can)

SUGAR AND SPICE TOPPING

2 tablespoons granulated sugar

½ teaspoon ground cinnamon

½ teaspoon ground nutmeg

9 x 5 x 3-INCH LOAF PAN

A lovely addition to a holiday table, but welcome any time of the year. Good solo or with Nutmeg-Honey Whipped Cream (page 161) or Pineapple–Golden Raisin Sauce (page 162).

Heat the oven to 325°F. Grease the pan.

Beat the butter, sugars, and vanilla with an electric mixer on high speed, until pale and fluffy.

Reduce the speed to medium. Add the eggs, one at a time, beating after each.

Reduce the mixer speed to low.

Beat in 1 cup of the flour, the baking powder, cinnamon, nutmeg, ginger, baking soda, salt, and cloves. Then add the pumpkin. The batter may look curdled.

When well blended, stir in the remaining flour until just incorporated. Do not overmix.

Spread the batter (5 cups) in the pan. Mix together the Sugar and Spice Topping ingredients and sprinkle on top.

Bake until a cake tester inserted in the center comes out clean, about 1 hour and 10 minutes.

Cool the cake in the pan on a wire rack for about 30 minutes. Loosen the edges and turn the cake out. Let cool completely. Wrap airtight. Store at room temperature no longer than 12 hours. After that refrigerate or freeze, or else the cake will spoil.

Raisin-Pumpkin Pound Cake

Use the same ingredients and pan as for Pumpkin Pound Cake (page 124), plus: ¾ cup dark raisins.

Follow the directions above, adding the raisins to the batter along with the pumpkin. Increase the baking time to 1 hour and 25 or 30 minutes, until the cake tests done, as described. Store as directed above.

Vanilla-Bean Vanilla Cake

12 Portions.

1 vanilla bean
1 cup granulated sugar
12 tablespoons (1½ sticks)
    unsalted butter,
    at room temperature
4 large eggs, at room tempera-
    ture
1 teaspoon baking powder

1 teaspoon vanilla extract
⅛ teaspoon salt
1¼ cups all-purpose flour; or
    1½ cups cake flour
9- TO 9½-INCH SPRINGFORM PAN
OR 9-INCH ROUND CAKE PAN
LINED WITH FOIL (SEE BELOW)

If you love vanilla, you'll love this sweet cake. It is petite—just about 1 inch high—but what it lacks in stature it makes up for in soothing, comforting vanilla flavor. Enjoy it with a small scoop of vanilla ice cream, or with slightly sweetened mashed strawberries. Sip espresso or a perfumy tea, such as Earl Grey or Lapsang souchong. But first, invest in a moist, good-quality vanilla bean. (Many vanillaphiles favor bourbon vanilla beans from Madagascar. Ask for them at spice or cookware stores.)

Use a springform pan if you have one; it eliminates the need to turn the cake upside down, disturbing the vanilla sugar topping. However, you can also line a 9-inch round cake pan with aluminum foil, leaving just enough foil extending over the edge so that you can lift out the foil and the cake with it.

Heat the oven to 325°F. Grease the pan or the foil. Snip tough ends off the vanilla bean and cut into ½-inch lengths.

Food processor method: Process the bean with the sugar for 5 minutes (yes, that long), until very finely chopped. Do not open the processor until the sugar dust has settled. To remove any remaining large chunks of vanilla bean, sift the sugar through a strainer onto a piece of wax paper. The sugar may be hot; let it cool for 4 or 5 minutes.

Blender method: Put the sugar in a blender and start the machine. Gradually drop in the chunks of vanilla bean. (Keep the container closed as much as possible, to contain the cloud of sugar.) When all of the chunks have been added, blend about 1 minute longer. Wait until the sugar settles, then sift and cool as directed above.

To make the cake: Set aside 2 tablespoons of the vanilla sugar for the topping. Mix the butter and the remaining vanilla sugar with an electric mixer, then beat on high speed for about 5 minutes, until pale and fluffy. Reduce the speed to medium. Add the eggs, one at a time, beating after each. Turn the mixer to low. Beat in the baking powder, vanilla, and salt. Add the flour, about one-third at a time, mixing only until blended.

Spread the batter (3½ to 4 cups) evenly in the pan. Bake 25 minutes. Moving the cake as little as possible, sprinkle the reserved 2 tablespoons vanilla sugar over the surface. Continue to bake until the cake is a deep golden brown and a cake tester inserted in the center comes out clean, about 15 minutes longer. (The sugar will change color, darkening slightly.)

Cool the cake in the pan on a wire rack for 15 to 20 minutes. Loosen the edges. Remove the springform sides and let the cake cool on the base, then loosen the bottom with a thin metal spatula and carefully slide the cake onto a plate. Or, lift the cake out of the pan by the foil. Carefully peel off the foil. Tightly wrapped, the cake keeps up to 1 week at room temperature; it also freezes well.

Brown Sugar–Brown Butter–Hazelnut Pound Cake

10 to 12 Portions

1 cup toasted hazelnuts or
pecans (page xxvii)

16 tablespoons (2 sticks)
unsalted butter

4 large eggs, at room temperature

1 cup packed dark brown sugar

1 teaspoon vanilla extract

¼ teaspoon salt

1 teaspoon baking powder

2 cups all-purpose flour

9 x 5 x 3-INCH OR 8½ x 4½ x
2¾-INCH LOAF PAN

Brown butter imparts a unique, rich, caramelly flavor to this cake, and the browning process turns the butter virtually into an oil. This cake is made very differently from most pound cakes, and as the technique involves cooking butter to a high temperature, just to be on the safe side, please invite small children and animals to leave the kitchen while you make the cake.

Heat the oven to 325°F. Grease the pan.

Finely chop the toasted hazelnuts or pecans with a knife or in a food processor.

Put the butter in a heavy 2- to 3-quart stainless steel saucepan over moderately high heat. Keeping one eye on the butter (once it melts, cooking time will be 5 to 6 minutes), crack the eggs into the bowl in which you will be making the batter. Add the sugar and beat with an electric mixer on high speed until thick and pale brown, about 4 minutes. Have ready a strainer and a glass 2-cup (or larger) measure. Now pay attention to the butter. A foam will appear on the surface and the butter will bubble merrily, big bubbles at first, then small ones, like a honeycomb. As the butter continues to cook, it will look crusty and awful but begin to smell wonderful, and the milk solids on the bottom of the pan will turn brown. If you have a candy or fat thermometer, use it. The butter is ready when it reaches 300°F. to 310°F., and looks clear and brown.

Remove the pan from the heat and pour the hot butter through the strainer into the cup measure. Then, with the mixer on medium speed, pour the hot butter—very carefully, so it doesn't splash—down the side of the bowl into the egg mixture in a steady stream, taking not more than 1 minute to add it all. Increase the speed to high and continue to beat about 2 minutes, while adding the vanilla and salt.

With the mixer on low, add the nuts and baking powder and beat about 15 seconds. Scrape the sides of the bowl. Add the flour, about ½ cup at a time, sprinkling it over the surface and not waiting until each amount is fully incorporated before you add the next. Scrape the sides of the bowl once or twice.

Spread the batter (4 cups) in the pan. Bake until a cake tester inserted in the center comes out clean, about 1 hour and 15 minutes. Cool the cake in the pan on a wire rack for 20 to 30 minutes. Loosen the edges and turn the cake out. Let cool completely. Store airtight a few hours or overnight at room temperature before serving or freezing.

Toasted Coconut and Almond
Pound Cake

12 Portions.

1½ loosely packed cups sweetened shredded or flaked
coconut (about 5 ounces)

1 cup whole almonds with
skins still on (about 5
ounces)

12 tablespoons (1½ sticks)
unsalted butter,
at room temperature

2¼ cups confectioners' sugar,
or 1¼ cups granulated sugar

1 teaspoon vanilla extract

¾ teaspoon almond extract

5 large eggs, at room temperature

1¼ teaspoons baking powder

¼ teaspoon salt

2¼ cups all-purpose flour, or
2⅓ cups cake flour

9 x 5 x 3-INCH LOAF PAN OR
9 x 3-INCH SPRINGFORM PAN

This cake speaks for itself, but if you feel an irresistible urge to serve it with something, sliced fresh oranges and/or vanilla or butter pecan ice cream will fill the bill. There's lots of texture in this cake from the coconut and almonds.

Heat the oven to 350°F. Coarsely chop the coconut and almonds in a food processor. Spread on a large pan with sides. Bake about 15 minutes, stirring four or five times, until lightly browned. Cool completely. (Tip the mixture onto a cookie sheet or even the countertop to speed cooling.)

Reduce the oven temperature to 325°F. Grease the baking pan.

Beat the butter, sugar, and extracts with an electric mixer on high speed, until pale and fluffy. Reduce the speed to medium. Add the eggs, one at a time, beating after each. Beat in the baking powder and salt. Scrape the sides of the bowl.

With the mixer on low, add the cooled toasted nuts. Scrape the sides of the bowl. Add the flour and mix until just incorporated. Do not overmix.

Spread the batter (5 cups) evenly in the pan. Bake until a cake tester inserted in the center comes out slightly moist, but the cake is springy to the touch and shrinks from the sides of the pan, about 1 hour.

Cool the cake in the pan on a wire rack for about 30 minutes. Loosen the edges. Turn the cake out from the loaf pan; or remove the springform sides, slide a thin metal spatula under the cake, and gently slide it onto the rack. Let cool completely. For best flavor, store airtight 1 day at room temperature before serving or freezing.

Pistachio-Ginger Pound Cake

12 Portions

6 ounces (1¼ cups) shelled pistachio nuts (see Note)
3 ounces crystallized ginger
1 cup granulated sugar
16 tablespoons (2 sticks) unsalted butter, at room temperature
4 large eggs, at room temperature

1¼ teaspoons ground ginger
1 teaspoon baking powder
¼ teaspoon salt
2 cups all-purpose flour, or 2½ cups cake flour
9 X 5 X 3-INCH LOAF PAN
FOOD PROCESSOR

Ginger brings out the subtle flavor of the pistachios.

Heat the oven to 325°F. Grease the pan.

Put the shelled pistachios in a small saucepan of boiling water and boil 1 minute. Drain the pistachios and place on one half of a linen or cotton dish towel. Fold the towel over the nuts and rub to loosen the skins. Peel off the brown skins.

Reserve 1 or 2 pieces of crystallized ginger to decorate the top of the cake. Put the sugar and the remaining crystallized ginger in a food processor. Process 1 to 2 minutes, until the ginger is finely chopped. The sugar will be rather damp. Add about half the pistachios and process briefly to chop. Scrape the mixture into the bowl in which you plan to make the batter.

Add the butter and beat with an electric mixer on medium speed, until well blended. Increase the speed to medium-high and add the eggs, one at a time, beating after each, and scraping the sides of the bowl two or three times.

Beat in the ground ginger, baking powder, and salt. With the mixer on low, add the flour and the remaining whole pistachios. Scrape the sides of the bowl two or three times, and beat only until the flour is just incorporated. Do not overmix.

Spread the batter (5 cups) evenly in the pan. Draw the handle of a rubber spatula once lengthwise through the batter 1 inch deep. (This will bake into an attractive split.) Slice the reserved crystallized ginger thin, and scatter or arrange it on top of the batter.

Bake until a cake tester inserted in the center comes out clean, about 1 hour and 10 to 20 minutes.

Cool the cake in the pan on a wire rack for about 30 minutes. Loosen the edges and turn the cake out. Let cool completely. For best flavor, store airtight 1 day at room temperature before serving or freezing.

NOTE: You may be able to buy pistachios that have been peeled as well as shelled. If so, they are ready to add to the food processor and the cake.

Festive Pound Cake

12 Portions

16 tablespoons (2 sticks)
  unsalted butter,
  at room temperature
2 cups granulated sugar, or 4
  cups confectioners' sugar
1 teaspoon vanilla extract
5 large eggs

½ teaspoon baking powder
2 cups all-purpose flour, or 2¼
  cups cake flour

9 X 5 X 3-INCH LOAF PAN

Expect to find a creamy, moist center when you slice through the crusty, slightly sunken top of this delicate cake. Its fine grain and sweet flavor go especially well with a glass of Champagne and a few strawberries for a festive occasion. A stand mixer with two bowls or a sturdy portable one works well here.

Heat the oven to 325°F. Grease the pan.

Put the butter and all but about ¼ cup of the granulated sugar or ½ cup of the confectioners' sugar in a large bowl. Add the vanilla. Set aside.

Crack open each egg, letting the whites drop into a deep, narrow bowl or electric mixer bowl, and putting the yolks in a separate small dish.

Beat the egg whites with an electric mixer on high speed, until soft peaks fold over when the beater is lifted. Sprinkle in the remaining ¼ cup granulated sugar or ½ cup confectioners' sugar and beat until the beaters leave a trail in the mixture.

Without washing the beaters, beat the butter and sugar on medium speed, until pale and fluffy. Slip in the yolks, one at a time, beating briefly after each. Beat in the baking powder and scrape the sides of the bowl. With the mixer on low, add the flour and beat until almost incorporated. Scrape the sides of the bowl. Add a big spoonful of the egg whites and beat it in to lighten the mixture. Add the remaining egg whites and fold in with a rubber spatula, just until incorporated.

Scrape the batter (5 cups) into the pan and smooth the surface. Draw the handle of a rubber spatula once lengthwise through the batter ½ inch deep. (This will bake into an attractive split.)

Bake until the top is a light golden brown and a cake tester inserted in the center comes out clean, about 1 hour and 15 minutes. Cool the cake in the pan on a wire rack for 30 minutes. Loosen the edges and turn the cake out. Let cool completely. For best flavor, store airtight 1 day at room temperature before serving or freezing.

Lemon-Mace Pound Cake

12 Portions

2 large lemons

1¼ cups granulated sugar

16 tablespoons (2 sticks)
   unsalted butter,
   at room temperature

2 teaspoons vanilla extract

4 large eggs, at room temperature

1 teaspoon baking powder

¼ plus ⅛ teaspoon ground
   mace

¼ teaspoon baking soda

¼ teaspoon salt

2 cups all-purpose flour

9 x 5 x 3-INCH LOAF PAN

Mace is a very close relative of nutmeg—in fact it is the lacy brown wrap around the small oval nutmeg. The amount of mace specified is just right. To measure ⅛ teaspoon, fill and level off ¼ teaspoon. Then, with the point of a knife, "cut" the mace across the middle and scoot half back into the jar. This cake is excellent with Plum Sauce (page 164) and Raspberry-Blueberry Sauce (page 163).

Heat the oven to 325°F. Grease the pan.

Scrub the lemons and pat dry. With a vegetable peeler, remove the brightly colored part of the peel and measure. You will need ⅓ cup lightly packed. Squeeze the lemons to make ⅓ cup juice.

Put the lemon peel and sugar in a food processor and process until the peel is very finely chopped. (Instead of using a food processor, you may grate the unpeeled lemons and add the peel to the sugar in the bowl.) The sugar will be very damp. Scrape the sugar mixture into the bowl in which you will be making the batter.

Beat the butter, the sugar mixture, and the vanilla with an electric mixer on high speed, until pale and fluffy.

Reduce the speed to medium. Add the eggs, one at a time, beating after each.

Beat in the lemon juice, baking powder, mace, baking soda, and salt (the batter will look curdled). Scrape the sides of the bowl often.

With the mixer on low, stir in the flour just until incorporated.

Spread the batter (5 to 6 cups) in the pan. Draw the handle of a spatula once lengthwise through the batter ½ inch deep. (This will bake into an attractive split.)

Bake until a cake tester inserted in the center comes out clean, about 1 hour and 5 to 10 minutes.

Cool the cake in the pan on a wire rack for about 30 minutes. Loosen the edges and turn the cake out. Let cool completely. For best flavor, store airtight 1 day at room temperature before serving or freezing.

Shirley Sarvis's Florentine Loaf

12 Portions

12 tablespoons (1½ sticks)
  unsalted butter,
  at room temperature
2⅔ cups confectioners' sugar
3 large eggs, at room temperature
⅓ cup yellow cornmeal
1 teaspoon vanilla extract

¼ teaspoon salt
½ cup golden raisins
1¼ cups cake flour, or 1 cup
  all-purpose flour
⅓ cup dark rum or sweet
  Marsala wine
9 x 5 x 3-INCH LOAF PAN

This may not be a cake you make for a party but, rather, one you make for a small gathering of appreciative friends. The cake has a crusty top that shatters when you cut it and it is deliciously wet in the middle. The raisins sink. But the taste is spectacular, like all of food and wine writer Shirley Sarvis's recipes. Reducing the sugar to 2 cups will cure the texture "problem." But it also "cures" the moist center I love.

Heat the oven to 325°F. Grease the pan. Line the pan with foil, letting it hang over the sides. Grease the foil.

Mix the butter and sugar in a large bowl with an electric mixer. When well blended, beat on high speed about 5 minutes, until pale and fluffy.

Reduce the speed to medium. Add the eggs, one at a time, beating after each. Add the cornmeal, vanilla, and salt. Beat to blend well. Scrape the sides of the bowl often.

With the mixer on low, stir in the raisins. Mix in about one third of the flour and half the rum or Marsala. As soon as they are about halfway mixed in, mix in the remaining flour and rum or Marsala. Scrape the sides of the bowl. Do not overmix.

Spread the batter (5 cups) evenly in the pan. Bake about 1 hour and 15 to 25 minutes. A sugary crust will form on top and a cake tester inserted in the center will come out with damp, sticky cake attached but not raw batter. Do not overbake.

Cool the cake in the pan on a wire rack for about 5 minutes. Loosen the edges, then let the cake cool completely in the pan. Lift the cake out of the pan by the foil. Carefully peel off the foil. For best flavor, store airtight 1 day at room temperature before serving or freezing.

Because they are made with oil instead of butter, chiffon cakes are relatively easy to put together. Essentially, the flour and other dry ingredients are mixed in a large bowl. Then the wet ingredients—water, oil, honey—are mixed in, along with egg yolks when called for. You can do all this mixing by hand with a wooden spoon in a large bowl and save your electric mixer (a portable electric one works fine here) for the egg whites. Lastly, the egg whites are beaten stiffly—slightly stiffer than for an angel food cake—and folded into the flour mixture.

Plan to make most of these cakes at least the day before you want to serve them because the flavors need that standing time to mellow and intensify. If you don't believe me, take a tiny piece from the bottom of a freshly baked and cooled cake and taste it. Compare it to the flavor a day or so later.

Chiffon cakes freeze well and take only an hour or two to thaw. Slice them while still frozen and they will thaw even faster.

Chiffon Cakes

JOANNAROY

Orange and Lemon Chiffon Cake

16 Portions

2 lemons
1 or 2 navel oranges
2 cups all-purpose flour
1½ cups granulated sugar
1 tablespoon baking powder
½ cup extra-virgin olive oil

1 cup egg whites (see page xxviii if you need help)
½ teaspoon salt
10 x 4-INCH TUBE PAN (A REMOVABLE BOTTOM IS HELPFUL)

This has an absolutely delightful flavor, and no one will guess that it is made with extra-virgin olive oil or that the egg yolks found in a traditional chiffon cake have been dispensed with. Do use extra-virgin or virgin olive oil; it makes a serious contribution to the overall flavor. The cake looks pretty sprinkled with confectioners' sugar before serving.

Heat the oven to 325°F. If the pan has a removable bottom, do nothing to it. If it does not, lightly grease the bottom (page xx). Line the bottom with wax paper or parchment paper cut to fit, and lightly grease the paper.

Scrub and dry the lemons and oranges. Grate the colored part of the peel, taking care not to grate any bitter white part, until you have (loosely packed) 1 tablespoon grated lemon peel and 2 teaspoons grated orange peel (see Note). Juice the fruit and measure ½ cup orange juice and ¼ cup lemon juice.

Put the flour, 1 cup of the sugar, and the baking powder into a large bowl. Stir to mix well. Add the oil, fruit juices, and grated peel. Beat smooth with a wooden spoon.

Put the egg whites and salt in a deep narrow bowl and beat with an electric mixer on medium-high speed, until they lose their yellow cast, greatly increase in volume, and begin to turn very white.

While still beating, sprinkle in the remaining ½ cup of sugar, about 2 tablespoons at a time. The whites will become very thick and very white and the beaters will leave a deep trail.

Whisk or beat about one eighth of the whites into the flour mixture. With a large metal spoon or rubber spatula, fold or gently stir in the remaining whites.

When well blended, pour the batter (8 cups) into the pan.

Bake until golden brown, springy to the touch, and a cake tester inserted in the center of the cake comes out clean, 50 to 55 minutes.

Turn the pan upside down on a wire rack. If the cake has baked higher than the rim of the pan, turn the pan upside down onto a beer or soda bottle (the bottle goes in the hollow tube). Leave on the countertop until the cake is completely cold. Loosen the edges (and tube) with a knife. Turn out the cake, loosen and remove the pan bottom, or peel off the paper. Serve freshly baked, or store airtight 1 day at room temperature before serving or freezing.

NOTE: Instead of grating the peel you can remove the peel of the lemons and one of the oranges with a vegetable peeler. Put them into a food processor or blender with the 1 cup of sugar and process 3 or 4 minutes (yes, that long) until chopped as fine as possible. The sugar will be moist. Add it with the oil, not the flour. Be sure not to try to whip it with the egg whites, because the citrus oils will deflate them.

Chocolate-Orange Chiffon Cake

16 Portions

2 navel oranges

3 ounces semisweet chocolate

2 cups all-purpose flour

1½ cups granulated sugar

1 tablespoon baking powder

½ cup extra-virgin olive oil

1 cup egg whites (see page xxviii if you need help)

½ teaspoon salt

10 X 4-INCH TUBE PAN (A REMOVABLE BOTTOM IS HELPFUL)

Heat the oven to 325°F. If the pan has a removable bottom, do nothing to it. If it does not, lightly grease the bottom (page xx). Line the bottom with wax paper or parchment paper cut to fit, and lightly grease the paper.

Scrub and dry the oranges. Grate the colored part of the peel, taking care not to grate any bitter white part, until you have (loosely packed) 4 teaspoons grated orange peel (see Note). Juice the oranges and measure ¾ cup.

Grate the chocolate or chop in a small food processor.

Put the flour, 1 cup of the sugar, the chocolate, and the baking powder into a large bowl. Stir to mix well. Add the oil, orange juice, and grated peel. Beat smooth with a wooden spoon.

Put the egg whites and salt in a deep narrow bowl and beat with an electric mixer on medium-high speed, until they lose their yellow cast, greatly increase in volume, and begin to turn very white.

While still beating, sprinkle in the remaining ½ cup of sugar, about 2 tablespoons at a time. The whites will become very thick and very white and the beater will leave a deep trail.

Whisk or beat about one eighth of the whites into the flour mixture. With a large metal spoon or rubber spatula, fold or gently stir in the remaining whites.

When well blended, pour the batter (7 to 8 cups) into the pan.

Bake until golden brown, springy to the touch, and a cake tester inserted in the center of the cake comes out clean, about 50 to 55 minutes.

Turn the pan upside down on a wire rack. If the cake has baked higher than the rim of the pan, turn the pan upside down onto a beer or soda bottle (the bottle goes in the hollow tube). Leave on the countertop until the cake is completely cold. Loosen the edges (and tube) with a knife. Turn out the cake, loosen and remove the pan bottom, or peel off the paper. Serve freshly baked, or store airtight 1 day at room temperature before serving or freezing.

NOTE: Instead of grating the peel you can remove the peel of the oranges with a vegetable peeler. Put it into a food processor or blender with the 1 cup of sugar and process 3 or 4 minutes (yes, that long), until chopped as fine as possible. The sugar will be moist. Add it with the oil, not the flour. Be sure not to try to whip it with the egg whites.

Chiffon Spice Cake

16 Portions

2 cups all-purpose flour

1½ cups granulated sugar

1 tablespoon baking powder

1 teaspoon ground cloves

1 teaspoon ground cinnamon

¼ teaspoon freshly ground
    black pepper

¾ cup apple juice or cider

½ cup extra-virgin olive oil

1 tablespoon vanilla extract

1 cup egg whites (see page
    xxviii if you need help)

½ teaspoon salt

10 x 4-INCH TUBE PAN (A REMOV-
ABLE BOTTOM IS HELPFUL)

Heat the oven to 325°F. If the pan has a removable bottom, do nothing to it. If it does not, lightly grease the bottom (page xx). Line the bottom with wax paper or parchment paper cut to fit, and lightly grease the paper.

Put the flour, 1 cup of the sugar, the baking powder, cloves, cinnamon, and pepper into a large bowl. Stir to mix well. Add the apple juice or cider, the oil, and the vanilla. Beat smooth with a wooden spoon.

Put the egg whites and salt in a deep narrow bowl and beat with an electric mixer on medium-high speed, until they lose their yellow cast, greatly increase in volume, and begin to turn very white.

While still beating, sprinkle in the remaining ½ cup of sugar, about 2 tablespoons at a time. The whites will become very thick and very white and the beater will leave a deep trail.

Whisk or beat about one eighth of the whites into the flour mixture. With a large metal spoon or rubber spatula, fold or gently stir in the remaining whites.

When well blended, pour the batter (7 to 8 cups) into the pan.

Bake until golden brown, springy to the touch, and a cake tester inserted in the center of the cake comes out clean, about 50 to 55 minutes.

Turn the pan upside down on a wire rack. If the cake has baked higher than the rim of the pan, turn the pan upside down onto a beer or soda bottle (the bottle goes in the hollow tube). Leave on the countertop until the cake is completely cold. Loosen the edges (and tube) with a knife. Turn out the cake, loosen and remove the pan bottom, or peel off the paper. Serve freshly baked, or store airtight 1 day at room temperature before serving or freezing.

Walnut-Date Chiffon Cake

12 to 16 Portions

1 cup all-purpose flour

1 cup granulated sugar

1 teaspoon baking powder

½ teaspoon ground cardamom

¼ teaspoon salt

¼ teaspoon baking soda

One 8-ounce package pitted
   dates

1 cup walnuts, coarsely
   chopped

½ cup water

¼ cup vegetable or mild olive
   oil

¼ cup mild or dark molasses

3 large eggs

10 x 3-INCH ROUND CAKE PAN OR
10 x 4-INCH TUBE PAN (A REMOV-
ABLE BOTTOM IS HELPFUL)

The walnuts and dates usually form a layer on the bottom of the cake.

Heat the oven to 325°F. If the pan has a removable bottom, do nothing to it. If it does not, lightly grease the bottom (page xviii). Line the bottom with wax paper or parchment paper cut to fit, and lightly grease the paper.

In a large bowl, mix the flour, ¾ cup of the sugar, the baking powder, cardamom, salt, and baking soda. Stir with a wooden spoon to mix well.

Chop the dates, or cut them into small pieces with oiled scissors; you should have just about 2 cups. Add the dates and the walnuts to the bowl and toss with your fingers to mix and coat with flour.

Add the water, the oil, and molasses. Separate the egg yolks from the whites (see page xxviii if you need help), dropping the yolks into the oil and water and putting the whites into a deep narrow bowl. Stir the flour mixture until smooth and well blended.

Beat the egg whites with an electric mixer on medium-high speed until they lose their yellow cast, greatly increase in volume, and begin to turn very white.

While still beating, sprinkle in the remaining ¼ cup of sugar, about 2 tablespoons at a time. The whites will become very thick and very white and the beater will leave a deep trail.

Whisk or beat about one eighth of the whites into the flour mixture. With a large metal spoon or rubber spatula, fold or gently stir in the remaining whites.

Pour the batter (5 to 6 cups) into the pan. Bake until a cake tester inserted in the center comes out fairly clean but with no uncooked batter sticking to it, and the cake is springy to the touch, about 1 hour.

Turn the pan upside down on a wire rack until cake is completely cold. Loosen the edges (and tube) with a knife. Turn out the cake, loosen and remove the pan bottom, or peel off the paper. Store airtight 1 to 2 days at room temperature before serving or freezing.

Kumquat-Almond Chiffon Cake

10 to 12 Portions

½ pound kumquats (about 2 cups or 24 kumquats), stems removed

1 cup almonds (blanched, unblanched, slivered—whatever, doesn't matter)

2 cups granulated sugar

½ cup vegetable or mild olive oil

5 large eggs, yolks and whites separated (see page xxviii if you need help)

2 teaspoons baking powder

¼ teaspoon baking soda

1½ cups all-purpose flour

10 X 4-INCH TUBE PAN (A REMOVABLE BOTTOM IS HELPFUL)

FOOD PROCESSOR

This small, moist cake is a great reason to rescue those festive little citrus fruits before they dehydrate in the fruit bowl.

Put the kumquats in a small saucepan and cover with cold water. Bring to a boil. Cover and simmer 20 to 25 minutes over low heat, until the kumquats are tender when pierced. (This can be done a day or two ahead.) Drain, reserving ¼ cup cooking liquid, and cool the kumquats.

Heat the oven to 325°F. If the pan has a removable bottom, do nothing to it. If it does not, lightly grease the bottom (page xx). Line the bottom with wax paper or parchment paper cut to fit, and lightly grease the paper.

Put the almonds and 1½ cups of the sugar into a food processor and process for 1 to 2 minutes, until the nuts are very finely chopped.

Add the ¼ cup kumquat cooking liquid to the processor, along with the oil and egg yolks.

Remove any seeds from the kumquats, and drop the fruit into the food processor. Process until the kumquats are chopped fine. Sprinkle the baking powder and baking soda and then the flour over the surface. Process to mix in, scraping the sides of the bowl once or twice.

In a large bowl, beat the egg whites with an electric mixer on medium-high speed, until the whites lose their yellow cast, greatly increase in volume, and begin to turn white. While still beating, sprinkle in the remaining ½ cup sugar, about 2 tablespoons at a time. The whites will turn very white and glossy, and the beater will leave a deep trail.

Spread about one eighth of the beaten whites over the surface of the kumquat mixture. Turn the processor on/off four or five times to incorporate the whites.

Scrape the kumquat mixture into the bowl of whites and fold in just until blended. Scrape the batter (8 cups) into the pan. Bake until a cake tester inserted in the center of the cake comes out fairly clean— cooked but not raw batter clinging to it is okay—and the cake feels springy to the touch, about 1 hour and 15 minutes.

Place the pan on a wire rack and let the cake cool completely. Loosen the edges (and tube) with a knife. Turn out the cake, loosen and remove the pan bottom, or peel off the paper. Store airtight 1 to 2 days at room temperature before serving or freezing.

Coffee-Hazelnut Honey Cake

16 to 20 Portions

2½ cups all-purpose flour

½ cup granulated sugar

1 tablespoon baking powder

½ teaspoon baking soda

¼ teaspoon salt

1 teaspoon ground cardamom

1½ cups golden raisins (7½ to 8 ounces)

1 cup toasted hazelnuts (page xxvii), coarsely chopped

½ cup water

2 tablespoons instant coffee granules

5 large eggs

1¼ cups honey (1 pound)

½ cup vegetable or mild olive oil

2 tablespoons mild or dark molasses

10 x 4-INCH TUBE PAN OR 10 x 3-INCH ROUND CAKE PAN (A REMOVABLE BOTTOM IS HELPFUL)

You can use pecans or almonds instead of hazelnuts, and ½ cup packed brown sugar instead of the granulated sugar and molasses. You may also replace the water and instant coffee granules with ½ cup of brewed espresso. Make this cake at least 2 days before you need it. The egg whites are not beaten separately as they are in most chiffon cakes.

Heat the oven to 325°F. If the pan has a removable bottom, do nothing to it. If it does not, lightly grease the bottom (page xx). Line the bottom with wax paper or parchment paper cut to fit, and lightly grease the paper.

Put the flour, sugar, baking powder, baking soda, salt, and cardamom into a large bowl. Stir to mix well. Add the raisins and hazelnuts. Toss to coat with the flour.

Mix the water and the coffee granules and stir until the coffee is dissolved. Add to the flour mixture along with the eggs, honey, oil, and molasses. Beat with an electric mixer or wooden spoon until well blended.

Scrape the batter (6 to 7 cups) into the pan. Bake until the cake feels springy to the touch and a cake tester inserted in the center of the cake comes out clean, 1 hour and 10 to 15 minutes.

Place the pan upside down on a wire rack to cool at least 30 minutes. Loosen the edges (and tube) with a knife. Turn out the cake, loosen and remove the pan bottom, or peel off the paper. Store airtight at least 2 days at room temperature before serving or freezing.

Mocha Chiffon Cake

12 Portions.

¾ cup milk

3 ounces unsweetened chocolate, cut up

1 tablespoon instant coffee
granules

4 large eggs

1 cup all-purpose flour

1½ cups granulated sugar

1½ teaspoons baking powder

¼ teaspoon salt

⅓ cup vegetable oil

1 tablespoon vanilla extract

Confectioners' sugar

10 X 4-INCH TUBE PAN (A REMOV-
ABLE BOTTOM IS HELPFUL)

A very small cake, but full of flavor.

Put the milk, chocolate, and coffee granules in a heavy saucepan over very low heat. Heat, stirring occasionally, until the chocolate has melted. Remove from the heat and let cool. (To hasten cooling, sit the pan in cold water in the sink or in a bowl of ice water for a few minutes.)

Crack open the eggs, letting the whites drop into a deep narrow bowl and putting the yolks in a small dish. Let the whites come to room temperature (about 20 minutes).

Meanwhile, heat the oven to 325°F. If the pan has a removable bottom, do nothing to it. If it does not, lightly grease the bottom (page xviii). Line the bottom with wax paper or parchment paper cut to fit, and lightly grease the paper.

Mix the flour, 1¼ cups of the sugar, the baking powder, and salt in a large bowl.

Add the oil, the yolks, and the vanilla to the cooled chocolate mixture. Add the chocolate mixture to the flour mixture and stir to blend well.

Beat the egg whites with an electric mixer on medium-high speed until the whites lose their yellow cast, greatly increase in volume, and begin to turn white. While still beating, sprinkle in the remaining ¼ cup sugar, about 2 tablespoons at a time. The whites will turn very white and glossy, and the beaters will leave a deep trail.

Beat about one eighth of the beaten whites into the flour mixture. Then gently stir or fold in the remaining whites with a rubber spatula or metal spoon.

Scrape the batter (6 cups) into the pan. Bake until a cake tester inserted in the center of the cake comes out clean, about 50 minutes to 1 hour.

Place the pan on a wire rack to cool for 30 minutes. Loosen the edges (and tube) with a knife. Turn out the cake, loosen and remove the pan bottom, or peel off the paper. Store airtight 1 to 2 days at room temperature before serving or freezing. Sift confectioners' sugar over the top before serving.

New York Carrot Cake

12 Portions

1½ to 2 cups peeled carrots cut in ½-inch lengths

2 tablespoons grated or diced, peeled fresh gingerroot

1 cup granulated sugar

½ cup vegetable oil

¼ cup orange juice or water

¼ cup mild molasses

3 large eggs

1 cup toasted hazelnuts (page xxvii)

1¼ cups all-purpose flour

1½ teaspoons baking powder

1 teaspoon ground cinnamon

½ teaspoon salt

⅓ cup golden raisins

10 x 4-INCH TUBE PAN (A REMOVABLE BOTTOM IS HELPFUL)

FOOD PROCESSOR

Hazelnuts and ginger turn country mouse carrot cake into a petite city slicker.

Heat the oven to 325°F. If the pan has a removable bottom, do nothing to it. If it does not, lightly grease the bottom (page xx). Line the bottom with wax paper or parchment paper cut to fit, and lightly grease the paper.

Put the carrots and ginger into a food processor and process several seconds, until finely chopped.

Add ¾ cup sugar, oil, juice, or water, and the molasses.

Crack open the eggs, letting the whites fall into a deep narrow bowl and adding the yolks to the processor. Process briefly to mix.

Add the hazelnuts and turn the processor on/off four or five times to coarsely chop them. Scrape the sides of the bowl. Sprinkle the flour, baking powder, cinnamon, and salt over the surface; turn the machine on/off four or five times and then scrape the bowl sides.

Add the raisins. Turn on/off two or three more times to mix them in. Scrape the bowl sides.

Beat the egg whites with an electric mixer on medium-high speed until they lose their yellow cast, greatly increase in volume, and begin to turn very white. Beat in the remaining ¼ cup sugar, about 2 tablespoons at a time. The whites will turn very white and glossy, and the beaters will leave a deep trail.

Spread about one eighth of the beaten whites on top of the mixture in the work bowl. Turn the processor on/off three or four times to incorporate the whites.

Scrape the contents of the work bowl into the bowl of beaten whites and fold or gently stir with a rubber spatula or metal spoon, just until blended in.

Scrape the batter (6 cups) into the pan. Bake until the cake is springy to the touch and a cake tester inserted in the center comes out clean, about 1 hour. Place the pan on a wire rack to cool for 1 hour or longer. Loosen the edges (and tube) with a knife. Turn out the cake, loosen and remove the pan bottom, or peel off the paper. Store airtight 1 to 2 days at room temperature before serving or freezing.

Instead of frostings, I have included a selection of delicious toppings, ranging from heavenly Nutmeg-Honey Whipped Cream (page 161) to Caramel Apples (page 165). There's also a Superb Chocolate Sauce (page 166). A slice of cake with a spoonful of sauce alongside is more enjoyable and, to me, seems more stylish and contemporary than a frosted cake.

When a cake does seem bare on top, sift a little confectioners' sugar over it. Keep a filled sugar dredger handy. A dredger looks like a tin can with a handle on the side and holes in the top and can be found at cookware shops.

Toppings and Sauces
for Cakes

JOANNA ROY

Chocolate Whipped Cream

2 Cups

2 ounces semisweet and
 1 ounce unsweetened
 chocolate, or
3 ounces bittersweet
 chocolate

3 tablespoons water
1 cup heavy (whipping) cream
1 tablespoon granulated sugar
½ teaspoon vanilla extract

To double up the chocolate experience, serve this with Intense Chocolate Tea Bread (page 38) or Hazelnut-Chocolate Angel Food Cake (page 94).

Chop the chocolate, then melt it with the three tablespoons water in a 1- to 2-quart heavy saucepan over low heat, stirring frequently until smooth. Remove from the heat and cool until the chocolate is cool to the touch but not cold.

Whip the cream with an electric mixer on high speed until it begins to thicken. Add the melted chocolate, sugar, and vanilla and whip until soft peaks form when the beater is lifted. Watch carefully so the cream doesn't turn into butter.

Serve right away or chill for up to 3 hours.

Mocha Whipped Cream

Prepare Chocolate Whipped Cream (above) as directed, adding ¼ teaspoon powdered instant espresso coffee to the cream along with the chocolate, sugar, and vanilla.

Nutmeg-Honey Whipped Cream

About 2 Cups

1 cup heavy (whipping) cream
1 tablespoon plus 1 teaspoon
   honey
⅛ teaspoon ground nutmeg

Good with Tennessee Whiskey Cake (page 114).

Whip the cream with an electric mixer on high speed until it begins
to thicken. Add the honey and the nutmeg and continue whipping
until soft peaks form when the beater is lifted.

Serve right away or chill for up to 1 hour.

Pineapple–Golden Raisin Sauce

1½ Cups

1 tablespoon unsalted butter
⅓ cup packed light brown
   sugar
⅓ cup cold unsweetened
   pineapple juice

1½ cups peeled, cored, and
   diced fresh pineapple
   (¼-inch dice)
⅓ cup golden raisins
1 teaspoon cornstarch

This sauce makes a nice addition to Pumpkin Pound Cake (page 124) or Chiffon Spice Cake (page 128). And for a steamy winter dessert, try it with Molasses Ginger Cake (page 44).

Melt the butter in a medium-size nonstick skillet over moderate heat. Stir in the sugar and 1 tablespoon of the pineapple juice and cook until bubbly.

Add the diced pineapple and raisins to the sugar mixture, reduce the heat to low, and simmer about 8 minutes, stirring occasionally, until the pineapple is tender and translucent.

Mix the remaining pineapple juice with the cornstarch until smooth. Stir into the mixture in the skillet. Increase the heat slightly and stir until boiling. Simmer 1½ to 2 minutes. Remove from the heat. Serve warm.

Raspberry-Blueberry Sauce

2 Cups

2 cups fresh or unsweetened
    frozen raspberries
⅓ cup raspberry preserves or
    jam
⅓ cup water

2 tablespoons granulated
    sugar
1 cup fresh or frozen blue-
    berries (small berries
    work better here)

Wonderful with Lemon-Mace Pound Cake (page 136). Be sure to use a good-quality preserve.

Mix 1 cup of the raspberries, the preserves, water, and the sugar in a medium-size heavy saucepan (not uncoated aluminum). Bring to a boil over moderately high heat, mashing the raspberries with a wooden spoon. Boil 1 minute. Remove from the heat.

Strain the raspberry mixture through a fine strainer suspended over a bowl, pressing down on raspberries to release the juices. Discard the seeds.

Stir the blueberries and the remaining 1 cup raspberries into the hot raspberry syrup. Cover and let stand until cool. Refrigerate until ready to use.

Plum Sauce

About 2⅓ Cups

1¼ to 1½ pounds ripe tart red plums, such as Santa Rosa plums (about 8 small plums) ¾ cup granulated sugar (try ⅔ cup if plums are very sweet)	One 3-inch cinnamon stick, broken in half, or ⅛ teaspoon ground cinnamon Pinch of ground cloves

Also good with Lemon-Mace Pound Cake (page 136).

Halve and pit the plums. Cut each half into 4 or 6 wedges. You should have 3½ to 4 cups.

Mix all ingredients in a medium-size heavy saucepan. Cover and bring just to a simmer over moderate heat, stirring every couple of minutes. The plums will release liquid that mixes with and dissolves the sugar.

Reduce the heat to low and simmer 4 to 6 minutes, until the plums are hot and soft. Remove from the heat. (The plums will continue to cook slightly.)

Remove the cinnamon stick. Serve sauce warm or chilled.

Caramel Apples

About 2 Cups

3 tablespoons unsalted butter	1¼ pounds Granny Smith
⅓ cup packed dark brown sugar	apples, peeled, cored, and cut into ¼-inch-thick wedges (about 4 cups)

Fabulous with one of the plainer cakes or with Brown Sugar Angel Food Cake (page 80).

Melt the butter in a large nonstick skillet over moderately high heat. Stir in the sugar and cook 1 to 2 minutes, stirring frequently until well blended and bubbly.

Add the apples to the sugar mixture and toss with two wooden spoons until well coated. Reduce the heat to low, cover, and cook about 20 minutes, stirring every 4 or 5 minutes and pushing the apples down into the syrup, until the apples are tender and translucent.

Remove from the heat. Serve warm.

Superb Chocolate Sauce

About 1½ cups.

1 cup heavy (whipping) cream
6 ounces bittersweet or semisweet chocolate,
      coarsely chopped

2 tablespoons unsalted butter
1 tablespoon granulated sugar

Try a small spoonful with Caramel-Coffee Angel Food Cake (page 84), Miriam's Sour Cream Pound Cake (page 108), or Festive Pound Cake (page 134).

Put all the ingredients in a medium-size heavy saucepan. Stir over low heat until the chocolate is melted. Serve hot.

VARIATIONS

Add 1 tablespoon Cognac.
Add 1 teaspoon vanilla extract.

Index